FIRST IN BUSINESS • FIRST IN TALK
2200 FLETCHER AVENUE
FORT LEE, NEW JERSEY 07024

Dear Reader,

My years of experience as a financial journalist have taught me one thing: the failure to take control of one's finances guarantees an uncertain and perhaps even perilous financial future. Sadly, too many Americans are living solely for today and are setting themselves up for a financial disaster some time in the future.

I wrote *10 Steps to Financial Prosperity* in the hopes of encouraging people to start thinking about their futures and, most importantly, TO DO SOMETHING ABOUT IT!

To help you to take the critical action steps to gain control of your financial future, I have enclosed a computer disk with the book. The disk shows you how to track expenses, how much to save to reach your long-term goals and even how to write your own will. It's simple and easy-to-use, even for computer amateurs like myself. Just follow the step-by-step instructions in the appendix. The main sections on the disk are:

- Your budget worksheet
- Your monthly budget
- Your child's college fund
- Your will
- Your retirement nest egg

I sincerely hope the book and computer disk will give you the tools you need to take charge of your financial destiny. As I think you'll find, it's just a matter of developing a sound plan and sticking to it.

Good luck on your road to financial prosperity.

Regards,

Bill Griffeth

P.S. A two cassette, abridged version of *Bill Griffeth's 10 Steps to Financial Prosperity* is available for $17.95 from Dove Audio at fine bookstores everywhere or call TOLL FREE 1-800-328-DOVE.

A Service of NBC

Bill Griffeth's

10
Steps
to Financial
Prosperity

*CNBC Award
Winning Anchor
Shows You
How to Achieve
Financial
Independence*

PROBUS PUBLISHING COMPANY
Chicago, Illinois
Cambridge, England

© 1994, William C. Griffeth

ALL RIGHTS RESERVED. No part of this publication may be reproduced, stored in a retrieval system, or transmitted, in any form or by any means, electronic, mechanical, photocopying, recording, or otherwise, without the prior written permission of the publisher and the copyright holder.

This publication is designed to provide accurate and authoritative information in regard to the subject matter covered. It is sold with the understanding that the author and the publisher are not engaged in rendering legal, accounting, or other professional service.

Authorization to photocopy items for internal or personal use, or the internal or personal use of specific clients, is granted by PROBUS PUBLISHING COMPANY, provided that the U.S. $7.00 per page fee is paid directly to Copyright Clearance Center, 222 Rosewood Drive, Danvers, MA 01923, USA; Phone: 1-508-750-8400. For those organizations that have been granted a photocopy license by CCC, a separate system of payment has been arranged. The fee code for users of the Transactional Reporting Service is 1-55738-575-0/94/$00.00 + $7.00.

ISBN 1-55738-575-0

Printed in the United States of America

BB

2 3 4 5 6 7 8 9 0

ZG

I dedicate this book to:

My family:

To my mother, Frances, and to the memory of my father, Charles, both of whom lovingly taught me the true value of a dollar.

To my wife, Cindy, and our children, Chad and Carlee, who support me with love and incredible patience.

My friends:

To *The Six Pack*, especially Tim and Debbie. I wrote this book with you in mind.

To Rusty and Wendy, who are already financially prosperous.

My generation:

The Baby Boomers. If we start saving now, gang, we can finish life the way we started it: carefree and comfortable.

TABLE OF CONTENTS

ACKNOWLEDGMENTS

This book was a major team effort.

My thanks to the folks at Probus Publishing, first for having the faith that "just another pretty face on TV" could actually write a book, and second for their enthusiasm, their creativity, their professionalism, their flexibility, and the incredibly efficient way they put this book and computer disk together.

I also thank my colleagues at CNBC, many of whom were kind enough to volunteer names and information when they thought it might be helpful to me (it was!).

A special thanks to the network's publicity whiz, Jason Klarman, for his energy and ideas.

Next, I must thank my own personal Board of Editors, experts in their fields who reviewed various chapters. They were enormously helpful. They are, in alphabetical order:

On debt: Robert McKinley, President, RAM Research, Frederick, MD

On mutual funds: Don Phillips, Publisher, Morningstar Mutual Funds, Chicago, IL

On real estate: Suzanne Petruzel, Jackson-Cross Real Estate, Philadelphia, PA and Bob Pisani, CNBC

On insurance: Craig E. Smith, Executive Vice President, Dreyfus Service Corp., New York, NY

On saving for college: W. Gordon Snyder, Executive Vice President, Twentieth Century Mutual Funds, Kansas City, MO

And for reviewing the whole manuscript, I thank: Alex Crippen, CNBC; Alison Tepper, Knight-Ridder Financial News, Washington, D.C.; Cindy Griffeth: My permanent partner in crime.

I must also thank Greg Morris, of MarketArts, Inc. in Dallas, TX, who first suggested the idea for the accompanying computer disk.

And I acknowledge my longtime colleague Robert Metz, who once told me that the best way to learn about something was to write a book about it. Boy, were you right, Bob.

"The human race has had long experience and a fine tradition in surviving adversity. But we now face a task for which we have little experience, the task of surviving prosperity."

—*Alan Gregg*
  writing in the New York Times
  November 4, 1956

"The virtue of prosperity is temperance; the virtue of adversity is fortitude."

—*Francis Bacon*

Introduction

Why I Wrote This Book
And what is financial prosperity anyway?

I am a TV journalist. Since 1981, my beat has been money. Perhaps you have seen me on NBC's national business/talk cable channel, CNBC.

My job is to understand, and report, what is happening in the rapidly changing world of global economics and finance. So my personal finances ought to be in incredible shape, you say. Well...

Let me tell you a story:

In the fall of 1992, *Money* magazine asked me if I would be a guinea pig for a new service they were introducing. It was a sophisticated computerized financial planning program designed to evaluate a client's monthly budget, long-range financial goals, retirement plan, and estate plan. I agreed to participate.

Boy, did it open my eyes.

The cobbler's family wasn't exactly going shoeless, but it was clear that *this* business journalist didn't exactly have his financial house in order.

Our monthly budget was in pretty good shape, although our debt level was a bit high, and my wife and I had done a good job of starting a college savings plan for our two children. But our investment portfolio was too conservative, and our retirement plan needed work. A lot of work.

"The cobbler's family wasn't exactly going shoeless, but it was clear that this business journalist didn't exactly have his financial house in order."

The truth was my wife and I didn't have a retirement plan to speak of. All we had were vague notions about playing golf and painting and traveling. Yes, we had been dutifully putting money away in our employers' 401(k) plans, but we had no idea how much our retirement was going to cost, or whether we were saving enough to pay for it.

My wife and I were not unique in our lack of preparation. A Merrill Lynch study, released in early 1993, concluded that the members of the Baby Boom generation (the 77 million Americans born between 1946 and 1964) were only saving roughly a third of the amount they would need to maintain their preretirement standard of living.

And a study conducted for Oppenheimer Management found that almost half of all American households have absolutely no pension coverage. It concluded that if members of the Boomer generation did not dramatically increase their savings, they were likely to have less than 60 percent of the income they would need to stop working.

But wait: there's more. The Social Security Administration, which has been running a surplus for a number of years, is scheduled to start running a deficit in the year 2011. That is, not so coincidentally, the year the first wave of Boomers will hit retirement age. In the meantime, a study by the Investment Company Institute found that by the year 2000, Social Security will contribute only 15 cents to every retirement dollar.

Consider this book a call to arms with a single message: It is time each of us started thinking about our financial future.

"Financial prosperity means being in control of your money."

Corporate America's defined benefit pensions, which rewarded our parents and grandparents for years of loyal service by paying for their retirement, are being replaced by corporate retirement plans that we pay for.

And Social Security is dying a slow death that will probably render it useless in another 30 years.

Bottom line: We are on our own when it comes to paying for our retirement. And we are doing a lousy job of preparing for it.

How do we avert disaster? By achieving financial prosperity.

What Is Financial Prosperity?

Financial prosperity has little to do with your level of income. It has everything to do with what you do with that income. If I had to define it in a single sentence, I would say:

Financial prosperity means being in control of your money.

In practical terms, it means:

- *Keeping your debt levels low enough* to maintain spending flexibility.

• *Keeping your spending levels low enough* to meet your savings goals.

• *Keeping your savings levels high enough* to meet tomorrow's needs.

It means being prepared for emergencies by purchasing enough insurance. And it means being responsible enough to put an estate plan together that provides for your dependents in case something happens to you.

It means getting your financial act together.

"The 10 steps I outline for achieving financial prosperity are universal in their application to people of all age levels and tax brackets."

Let me emphasize that this is *not* just a retirement planning guide. Nor is it just for Baby Boomers. The 10 steps I outline for achieving financial prosperity are universal in their application to people of all age levels and tax brackets.

To be honest with you, I wrote this book for myself to help me figure out how I was going to effectively finance a comfortable retirement for my wife and myself, to save enough for a decent college education for our two children, and to still maintain our current lifestyle — all without robbing a bank.

I am not a CPA or a CFA or a CLU, which means I am not a *credentialed* financial expert. But I have been asking financial planners plenty of questions about managing money since 1981. And I've been paying attention to their answers.

This book is a compendium of what I've learned. I've written it for people who don't have a clue about how to start getting a handle on their finances and for people who simply need confirmation that they are on the right track.

I think you'll find it to be a pretty easy read. I've tried to leave out a lot of technical terms and complicated theories. I speak two languages: I'm fluent in Financial Expert, but my native tongue is Financial Novice. Consider this book a translation from one language to the other.

I am paid to think about other people's money and how they save it and invest it. And for some reason, it has only now occurred to me to start thinking about my own money.

That's what this book is about: my money, and your money, and how we must seize control of our financial future and save ourselves from a disaster worse than the Great Depression of the 1930s.

Do we want previous generations waving their index fingers at us, saying "We told you so"?

We do not!

The time to take action is now.

Step 1

Take Control of Your Money!
Set financial goals for yourself

Do you have control of your money? Don Calhoun has control of his.

His name may not be familiar, but you will probably recall what he did.

In the spring of 1993, during a Chicago Bulls basketball game, Don was selected to participate in a contest at halftime where, if he could throw the ball into the basket from all the way across court, he would win $1 million.

Don bounced the ball a few times and then heaved it from one end of the court to the other.

SWISH! Nothing but net.

The crowd went wild. The Chicago Bulls went wild (Michael Jordan rushed to hug him), and for a brief period during the summer of '93 Don Calhoun was a national celebrity.

The day after his profitable accomplishment, he was a guest on NBC's "Today Show." Bryant Gumbel asked him what he was going to do with the money. Don mentioned that he had a young daughter he wanted to send to college someday, and he said that he also wanted to attend college and perhaps start a business. So, he said, he would probably invest his money in mutual funds.

Here was a young man who had been a $5 an hour shipping clerk, and now he was guaranteed $50,000 a year for the next 20 years. If that had been me, under Don's circumstances, the first check would have found its way to a sports car dealership, a few clothing stores, a jewelry store, some fine restaurants, and a bookstore or two.

But when Don's first check arrived he put it in the bank, and he started learning all he could about investing.

"I'm not used to handling that much money," he explained to me during an interview on CNBC, "so I have to learn."

Don had a plan for his newfound wealth: Instead of allowing the money to determine what his lifestyle would be, he decided to let his lifestyle determine what he would do with the money.

He had some well-defined financial goals, and he had a plan that would allow him to achieve those goals.

How to Take Control of Your Money

Do you often find yourself running out of money a couple of days before payday? Do you wonder why you can't afford to buy a new car or take the vacation you want when other people who make as much money as you do can?

The problem may not be your level of income. It could be what you're *doing* with your income.

You must take control of your money, be aware of how and where you spend it, and ultimately give it more purpose.

An effective plan for your money encourages you to develop a set of priorities that helps you achieve your financial goals.

There are three things you can do with your money:

1) Spend it. In 1992, Madison Avenue spent $131 billion to encourage us to spend our money. And we did. Government statistics show that the average American that year spent roughly 95 percent of what he or she earned. But money should be spent within the context of a carefully crafted monthly budget. (That's what Chapter 2 of this book is all about.)

2) Save it. Some of your money should be set aside temporarily for:

- *Unexpected emergencies*, like the new battery your car suddenly needs.

- *Unexpected opportunities*, like the antique coffee table you discover that you absolutely must have in your living room.

- *Expected short-term financial goals*, which include goods and services you plan to pay for within one to three years, like a new car or refrigerator, a vacation, quarterly property tax bills, or semi-annual life and auto insurance premiums.

Your savings should be in a safe, interest-bearing account that you have ready access to. A money market account with check writing privileges offered by major brokerage houses or mutual fund companies are ideal.

Note: Be sure the money market account maintains a constant price of $1. If it doesn't — meaning the price of the account fluctuates — you will end up paying capital gains taxes on each check you write.

3) Invest it. Some of the money you earn each month should be salted away in order to meet long-term financial goals that are five or more years away. Long-term financial goals include a new home, retirement, and your child's college education.

Since you won't need the money for awhile, you can afford to take some risk and put it in investments that could provide a greater return and help you keep up with inflation. A combination of stocks and bonds would be appropriate here. (See Chapter 3 for a more thorough discussion about investing your money.)

An effective money plan includes carefully considered spending, savings, and investment levels. But before you can figure out how much you are allowed to spend and how much you need to save and invest, you must develop some short-term and long-term financial goals.

What Are Your Financial Goals?

Start with your short-term goals. Set up a four-column list on a piece of paper. (And remember, the list should include more than just your wish list of things like new cars and vacations. It should also include upcoming financial obligations, such as taxes and insurance premiums.)

In the first column, write down the goal. In the second column, write down how much you believe it will cost. In the third column, write down the date of either when the financial obligation is due or when you would like to buy the car or take the vacation. Finally, in the fourth column, write down how much money you will need to save per month between now and the date you listed in column three.

SHORT-TERM FINANCIAL GOALS			
Goal	**Cost**	**When?**	**Savings/Mo.**
1) New car	$1,200	12 months	$100/mo.
2) Vacation	$2,000	8 months	$250/mo.
3) Car insurance	$600	6 months	$100/mo.
	Saving Needed Per Month:		$450.00

For example, I have listed three typical short-term goals. Let's say the car you want to buy in 12 months costs around $12,000, and you plan to make a 10 percent down payment. That means you will need to save about $100 a month over the next 12 months in order to achieve your goal (assuming you had no other savings at the time).

After you have completed your list, what happens if you find you can't save enough money each month to meet all of your short-term financial goals? You'll have to do one of two things:

1) *Reduce your price expectations.* (Plan, for example, to spend less on your vacation coming up in eight months.)

2) *Increase the amount of time before you achieve your goal.* (Delay the purchase of your new car for another six months.)

Obviously, for an upcoming contractual obligation like car insurance, you won't be able to do any adjusting.

SHORT-TERM FINANCIAL GOALS (*REVISED*)			
Goal	Cost	When?	Savings/Mo.
1) New car	$1,200	*18 months*	*$66/mo.*
2) Vacation	*$1,500*	8 months	*$187.50/mo.*
3) Car insurance	$600	6 months	$100/mo.
	Saving Needed Per Month:		*$353.50*

Now do the same thing for your long-term financial goals. Figuring out how much money to set aside for these is difficult if they are more than, say, 10 years down the road.

LONG-TERM FINANCIAL GOALS			
Goal	Cost	When?	Savings/Mo.
1) New House	$20,000*	5 years	$333/mo.
2) Retirement	????	30 years	????
3) Junior's College	????	15 years	????
* This represents a 10 percent down payment on a $200,000 home. To figure out how much you can actually afford to pay for a home at your income level, turn to Chapter 7.			
	Saving Needed Per Month:		????

The cost of retirement or a college education that won't occur for a number of years are both certainly moving targets. To determine how much you will need to save for retirement, turn to Chapter 6. To figure out how much you will need to save for your child's college education, turn to Chapter 10.

Certainly, you should try to save and invest as much of your monthly income as you can at all times, but realistically your priorities change depending on which financial phase of your life you are in.

The Financial Phases of Your Life

Each year, the Bureau of Labor Statistics asks thousands of Americans to keep diaries of how they spend their money. Here are the results from the 1992 survey[1]:

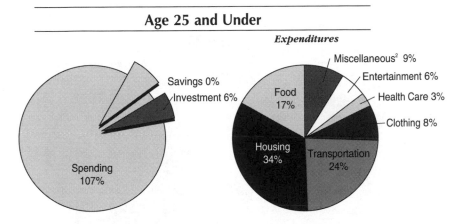

Age 25 and Under

Expenditures

This age group is understandably out of control when it comes to managing its money, especially when people this age are still in school. Textbooks and checkbooks don't mix. Long-term financial goals usually include next month's rent.

As you can see, the average person surveyed actually spent more than he or she earned. How is that possible? There are two explanations: Either 1) some of the

---

[1]This annual survey (See Appendix C at the end of the book for the full data.) only measures spending habits. Here is how I determined how much each age group saved and invested:

Savings. I simply subtracted each age group's average annual income from its average annual expenditures. I realize that the survey does not attempt to identify what each age group actually did with the income it did not spend, so I am using a basic economic assumption that any earnings not spent were saved.

Investment. I took this from the survey's Pension and Social Security category. It comes the closest to fitting my definition of "investment."

[2]I have lumped together eight small expenditure categories from the survey into Miscellaneous. They are: Alcoholic Beverages, Personal Care Products and Services, Reading, Education, Tobacco Products and Smoking Supplies, Cash Contributions, Life and Other Personal Insurance, and Miscellaneous.

money spent came out of already existing savings accounts, or 2) the money was borrowed, either from Mom and Dad or from some commercial lender.

Notice in the expenditure breakdown that this age group spends twice as much for entertainment as it does for health care. That will change with age.

Ages 25–34

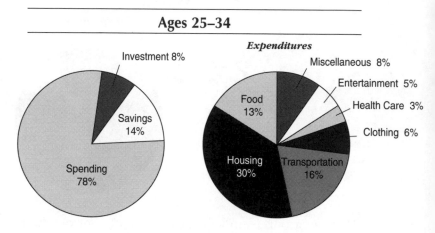

Consider this the accumulation phase of your life. Except for retirement, this is the period when you will spend the highest percentage of your income.

You're busy building a career, starting a family, and accumulating all the stuff you need. The emphasis right now is, quite understandably, on *spending* money. But saving is important here as well, because young people tend to load up on too much debt.

You will be doing yourself a huge favor if you start thinking about investing some money for long-term purposes. The earlier you start planning for retirement or a child's college education, the higher the quality of that retirement or education will be.

Ages 35–44

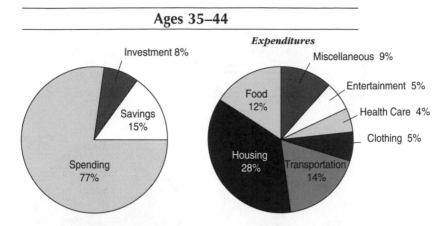

Expenditures

Investment 8%

Savings 15%

Spending 77%

Miscellaneous 9%

Entertainment 5%

Health Care 4%

Clothing 5%

Food 12%

Housing 28%

Transportation 14%

These are traditionally your peak earnings years. During this period, accumulation starts to slow down, and savings start to pick up.

And it's during this period that most people start to realize their own mortality and start preparing for retirement. A survey released in the fall of 1993 by the National Taxpayers Union Foundation found that, of those surveyed, 48 percent had begun to save for retirement before age 40. And another 19 percent started between ages 40 and 49.

Ages 45–54

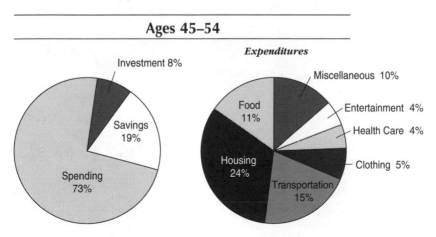

Expenditures

Investment 8%

Savings 19%

Spending 73%

Miscellaneous 10%

Entertainment 4%

Health Care 4%

Clothing 5%

Food 11%

Housing 24%

Transportation 15%

Now your retirement plans become more concrete. So it is probably no surprise that you save more of your income now than at any other time of your life.

Ages 55–64

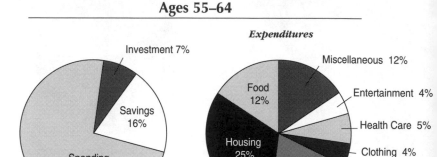

Now your retirement plans become more concrete.

It is during this period that the national average income begins to decline, either because people are starting to retire or they are forced to find another, lower-paying job.

It is also during this period that the amount of money spent on health care exceeds the amount spent on entertainment.

Age 65 and Beyond

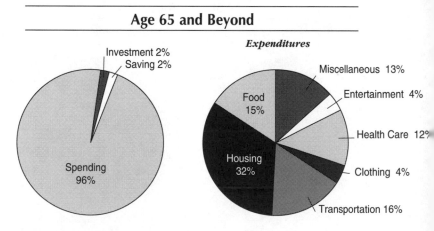

Welcome to retirement! Hopefully your health and bank account allow you the freedom to pursue your favorite activities.

Your financial priorities during retirement are different from when you were working. Notice how savings and investment drop dramatically during this period.

When you retire, probably your greatest concern is where your income will come from and how to preserve it.

Here is a breakdown of where the typical retired person's income came from in 1990:

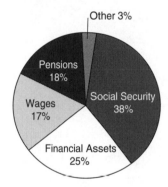

source: AARP

This retirement income distribution is expected to change dramatically over the next 15 to 30 years. Social Security's contribution, for example, is expected to decline quite a bit, especially after the Social Security Administration begins to run a deficit in the year 2011. The burden is expected to shift to pensions (both defined benefit pensions and defined contribution pensions) and to an individual's own financial assets and investments.

Wages may also play a greater role for retired people in the future. A survey released by Fidelity Investments in early 1994 showed that a surprising 80 percent of the investors polled expected to work part time during retirement, either to supplement their income or simply to give them something to do.

How do your spending, saving, and investment levels compare with the national averages? If you keep a written record of your monthly budget, it will be easy to determine.

If you don't keep a written record, Chapter 2 will show you how.

STEP 2

Budget-ize Yourself!
Assign a role to every dollar you earn

When I was in college, I dated a young woman who had a very simple method of budgeting herself. I have never forgotten it. Each payday she would cash her payroll check, take an old shoebox full of envelopes out of the closet, and fill each envelope with a preassigned amount of money until her entire paycheck had been distributed.

On the outside of one envelope she had written the word Rent: on another was written Groceries, another was marked Phone Bill, and so forth.

She also had an envelope labeled Entertainment, and whatever she assigned to that envelope was all she spent. She never dipped into one envelope to make up for a shortfall in another, unless there was a very, very good reason.

Her method was simple, her discipline made it work, and it got her through her financially lean college years.

Simply put, she had *budget-ized* herself.

To budget-ize yourself, all you have to do is *assign a role to each dollar you earn*. It is a very simple concept, but it is an extremely important one.

Three Kinds of Dollars

Assign the dollars you earn to one of three roles:

1) Deficit Dollars. These are the dollars you use to pay off your installment debt: your credit cards, your auto loans, any lines of credit you may have, or any personal notes.

2) Budget Dollars. These are the dollars you use to pay your monthly bills: your home mortgage or rent, your phone bill, your utilities bills, and so on.

3) Prosperity Dollars. These are the dollars you use to save for retirement, your child's college education, the future purchase of a home or other big ticket items, or for more immediate emergencies and opportunities.

Deficit Dollars Pay Yesterday's Bills.

Budget Dollars Pay Today's Bills.

Prosperity Dollars Pay Tomorrow's Bills.

At the end of 1993, here is what the average American did with every $100 in his or her paycheck:

- *$15.00 were Deficit Dollars.* In other words, they were using 15 percent of their monthly income to pay down installment debt.

- *$79.70 represented their Budget Dollars,* or the money used to pay their normal monthly expenses.

- *$5.30 represented their Prosperity Dollars.* That's it. Roughly 5 percent of their monthly income went to savings. And, by the way, that includes any money being invested in retirement plans like IRAs or 401(k)s.

Can You Do Better?

Of course you can. You should constantly be looking for ways to reduce the number of Deficit Dollars in your budget and to increase the number of Prosperity Dollars.

It is easier than you think.

I remember a family we profiled on CNBC who had set some goals for themselves. They wanted to save enough money to buy a nice home and two nice cars. They wanted to pay for college for their two children. And they wanted to save enough money so they wouldn't have to reduce their standard of living when they retired.

The kicker was they wanted to do it all on one income.

And they did it.

This family lived in a region of the northeast United States where the cost of living is quite high, so you would think it would take something close to a six-figure income to achieve all of their goals. But it didn't. The husband in this family was a salesman with a company that leased heavy equipment. His income was largely commission based. And it averaged between $60,000 and $65,000 a year.

The key to their success was their organized budget and their disciplined execution.

They had put together a list of goals that were important to them, and — just like my friend in college with her shoebox full of envelopes — they set up accounts for each of those goals. They put money in a bank account for the house and the cars, and they had money automatically deducted from the husband's paycheck and deposited in separate retirement and college accounts.

In their budget, those accounts were just as important as their rent payment and grocery money.

How to Budget-ize Yourself

I can remember many times when my wife and I sat down to create a monthly budget for ourselves. We would start by listing all of our normal monthly bills, and then we would write down what we thought we should be spending on each item.

By the next month, that "budget" was forgotten, and we were back to our old spending habits.

That's because the "budget" we had written down was not our budget. It was simply a budget that in no way reflected the reality of how we spent our money each month.

It was almost as if we were ashamed to acknowledge to ourselves that we spent money on more than the basic necessities of life.

Budget-izing yourself does *not* mean punishing yourself for spending money. Instead, it has two purposes:

- To help you determine where you actually spend your money.
- To help you spend your money more productively.

Have you ever joined a weight loss program? The first thing they usually have you do is to keep a diary of everything you eat for a month. The idea is that in order to set up an effective diet that works for you, you must first determine what you are actually eating and work from there.

You can use the same principle to budget-ize yourself. In order to put together an effective budget that gives you control over your money and meets all of your financial goals, you must first determine how and where you are actually spending your money.

To do that, keep a diary of your spending habits for three months. Organize it by dividing your expenses into the three ways you spend money:

- *Check writing.* This will include your monthly bills, such as your mortgage and utilities and the miscellaneous checks you write for whatever.

- *Cash.* Keep track of each time you make a trip to the automated teller machine to withdraw cash from your bank account. (When I kept my original budget diary, I didn't really worry about *what* my wife and I used the cash for. Instead, I just wanted to know *how much* cash we used each month.)

- *Credit card.* Don't be afraid to use your credit cards if they are a normal part of your monthly budget. You want your diary to be an accurate reflection of your spending habits.

Do this for three months. One month won't give you an accurate picture of your spending habits. You may have had some one-time, extraordinary expenses one month, or your expenses may have been unusually low another month. Three months will give you enough data to work with.

Then study your expenditure diary, and try to make sense of it:

—How many checks did you write each month, and what did you write them for? I was amazed at the number of checks my wife and I wrote. Many of them were for rather small amounts, but they added up in a big hurry.

"We made far too many unplanned purchases that ate up a number of checks, necessitated quick trips to the ATM for cash, and quickly added to the balances on our credit cards."

—How much cash did you spend each month, and how many trips did you make to your bank's automated teller machine? I found our cash spending to be the biggest drain on our monthly budget. We had to find a way to control it.

—How many times did you use your credit cards, and what did you use them for? When you buy something with a credit card, it doesn't *feel* like you're spending money. And because they represent a line of credit that neither drains your immediate cash flow nor demands immediate payment, credit cards are easy to use for impulsive "emergencies" like the antique table you didn't expect to buy, or the new outfit you just had to have.

Before we began to monitor our spending habits, the credit cards my wife and I carried were like loaded weapons ready to shoot down our monthly budget.

The biggest problem my wife and I had in all three payment categories was *impulse buying.* We made far too many unplanned purchases that ate up a number of checks, necessitated quick trips to the ATM for cash, and quickly added to the balances on our credit cards.

Just seeing it all on paper was enough to help us improve our spending habits. But to do the job, I set up a few basic goals for our budget:

1) Increase savings. Of course we wanted to save more each month. We always had. But now I was going to make Savings a category in our budget, just like Phone and Electricity. And after reviewing our previous, uncontrolled spending habits, I determined how much we could afford to save each month. So I set up a savings account, and started writing a check each month to that account.

2) Control our miscellaneous spending. This turned out to be the easiest part of putting our budget together. After we saw on paper exactly how much we had been "spending from the hip," we found it a very simple task to divert some of that money to savings and debt reduction.

3) Reduce our installment debt. I won't lie to you. At the time we put our budget together, my wife and I used four different credit cards, all with rather healthy balances. So one of my first goals was to eliminate two of the cards altogether and to lower the balances on the remaining two to more manageable levels.

Our Monthly Budget

It took a year, but my wife and I finally budget-ized the Griffeth household to the point where each dollar that came in left with a purpose. Our savings level is up, and our debt level is down. The key was accounting for every dollar we spent and eliminating our impulse buying. And, believe it or not, it was a pretty painless process.

To give you a better idea of what I'm talking about, Table 2-1 is the monthly budget my wife and I currently use. (See Appendix A.)

Table 2-1

MONTHLY BUDGET

Category	Budget	Actual	Actual
Prosperity Dollars			
My 401(k)	_____	_____	_____
Our Reserve Account	_____	_____	_____
Our Investment Account	_____	_____	_____
College Account #1	_____	_____	_____
College Account #2	_____	_____	_____
Budget Dollars			
Mortgage	_____	_____	_____
Phone	_____	_____	_____
Electricity/Water	_____	_____	_____
Gas	_____	_____	_____
Auto Fuel	_____	_____	_____
Cable TV	_____	_____	_____
Our Cash Allowance	_____	_____	_____
Our Checking Accounts	_____	_____	_____
Our Date	_____	_____	_____
Deficit Dollars			
Auto Loan #1	_____	_____	_____
Auto Loan #2	_____	_____	_____
Credit Card #1	_____	_____	_____
Credit Card #2	_____	_____	_____

Prosperity Dollars

These are the accounts where our savings and investment dollars go:

My 401(k) plan. This money is automatically deducted from my paycheck. I contribute the maximum allowed.

Our children's college funds. We have accounts set up for our two children through a family of mutual funds. The money is automatically deducted from my checking account each month.

Our reserve account. Each month we contribute a predetermined amount of money to a money market account with check writing privileges. It serves two purposes:

1) We use the money to pay periodic bills like auto and life insurance premiums, and expenses related to birthdays and Christmas.

2) We also use the money for emergencies or opportunities that come up periodically.

Our investment account. When we put our retirement plan together, we determined that the money being contributed to my 401(k) plan was simply not enough to meet our future financial goals. So I opened an account with a large discount brokerage firm, and I made arrangements for the automatic transfer of a predetermined amount of money from my checking account each month. I then decide where the money is invested.

This account serves two purposes:

- *Combined with our reserve account, it provides us with a financial cushion for emergencies.*

Between our reserve and investment accounts, I try to have six months' worth of our monthly expenses available.

- *It provides a greater return than a traditional savings account.* Yes, there is risk involved, and the money is not insured by the government, but I accept that, and I closely monitor the investments in the account.

Note: You should know, by the way, that my investment habits are governed by strict rules outlined by CNBC. I *must*, for example, hold any stock I purchase for at least four months (no short-term trading allowed). And I am not allowed to purchase any stock during the 48 hours after I have reported a story about it on the air. I am not allowed to trade options or futures, nor am I allowed to hold short positions in any stocks. Which is fine by me. I am, by nature, a buy 'em and hold 'em kind of value investor anyway.

Budget Dollars

This represents our basic monthly budget:

Mortgage. We pay our mortgage through an automatic deduction from my checking account.

Phone. We have a pretty high phone bill each month. We make a lot of long distance phone calls to our families in California, and my wife and I both have cellular phones that we use in our cars. If I ever needed to make some cuts in our monthly budget, this would be one of the first categories I would look at.

Utilities. In California, our utilities bills were pretty constant because of the stable weather. But now that we live on the East Coast, our utilities bills fluctuate quite a bit. Our electric bill, for example, is higher in the summer when we use the air conditioner, and our gas bill is a lot higher in the winter when we heat the house. So I adjust our budget targets as the seasons change.

Groceries. I can't believe how much food two small children eat!

Auto fuel. We have two oil company charge cards. One company is very prominent in the eastern part of the United States where we live. We obviously use that one the most. The other card is issued by a West Coast company, which we use during our frequent trips to California.

Cable TV. Since I work in cable TV, I am obviously a big supporter. But I honestly feel it is still too expensive. So we subscribe to our cable system's basic channel package and one premium channel, The Disney Channel. Our system also offers a pay-per-view movie service. But we don't use it, because it is still more expensive than our local video rental store.

Cash allowance. Before we put our formal budget together, my wife and I made frequent trips to our bank's automated teller machine whenever we needed the money. But without monitoring our withdrawals, we found that our cash spending was a volatile, unpredictable (and *large*) part of our monthly budget.

Now we make one trip to our bank's ATM every Friday, withdraw the same amount, and spend it as we each see fit. No more quick trips at odd hours.

Our check writing. My wife and I each have our own checking accounts. My paycheck is automatically deposited into my account, and then my wife electronically transfers a predetermined amount into her account. I pay the bills with my account, and then I allow myself a modest sum each month for trips to the hardware store, for example. My wife uses her account for grocery shopping, the many expenses related to our children, and miscellaneous (but necessary, I am assured!) shopping trips.

Our date.   My wife and I *try* to go on a date each Saturday evening. So we budget ourselves for a nice night on the town once a month, and then quiet evenings of dinner or a movie the other three Saturdays. (This looks great on paper, by the way, but let me assure you that with two young children it doesn't always work out.)

Deficit Dollars

This is the part of our budget devoted to installment debt:

Auto loans.   One of our loans is paid through an automatic deduction from my checking account. I would like to make payments the same way on the other loan, but that particular lender does not offer the service.

My wife and I generally hang on to our cars longer than the national average. And we try to stagger our purchases so that we have a two- to three-year period when one car is completely paid for so that we can save a few more dollars to put toward our next automobile purchase.

Credit cards.   We are now down to two major credit cards. One card is used for smaller purchases, and we only allow ourselves to charge a predetermined amount each month, which we then pay off each month.

We use the other card for larger purchases, like airline tickets for trips to California. We do not pay this card off each month. Instead, I make a predetermined payment toward the balance each month, and we never allow the balance to exceed the equivalent of 12 monthly payments (or one year's worth). And, if I ever needed to, I could always use either our reserve account or our investment account to pay off the whole balance. (See Chapter 5 for a more thorough discussion of credit card use.)

Automatic Payments

Automatic payments are a wonderful way to make your budget efficient and effective. As I pointed out before, in my budget I pay my mortgage and one auto loan through automatic deductions from my checking account. It makes paying the bills a lot easier. (This only works, by the way, for bills that involve a constant dollar amount each month.)

We also make automatic contributions to our investment account and our children's college accounts. It imposes an important discipline on us. If we don't actually handle the money, there is no temptation to use it for something else.

Be Flexible

In order for your budget to continue to serve you properly (remember: you're in control!), you must allow it to change.

Several months after we had put our budget together, my wife and I found that she consistently — and legitimately — needed more money for her checking account each month. So I took some money out of our reserve account, paid off one of our credit cards faster than I had originally planned, and that freed up enough funds each month to meet her needs.

A few months later, we found that we really could get by on less cash. So I reduced our weekly cash allowance and put the savings directly into our investment account.

"But don't completely deplete your savings in order to pay off debt."

Savings Versus Debt Reduction

A question that CNBC viewers frequently ask financial experts during our on-air call-in segments is, Which should get top priority: savings or debt reduction?

The experts most often tell people to pay down debt first. The interest you pay on debt (especially credit card debt) will most certainly be higher than any interest you earn on your savings. But don't completely deplete your savings in order to pay off debt. You should always have some savings cushion for emergencies.

TEN WAYS TO TURN DEFICIT DOLLARS INTO PROSPERITY DOLLARS

1) Cut down on impulse buying.

2) Use credit cards with more purpose. And if you carry a balance, shop around for the card with the cheapest interest rate.

3) Never pay retail for big ticket items. Shop around!

4) Use coupons when you shop for groceries. (And don't shop when you're hungry!)

5) Eat at home more often. Take a sack lunch to work once in awhile.

6) If you travel frequently, enroll in frequent flyer/hotel guest programs.

7) Vacation during the off-season. Rates are usually cheaper.

8) Pay yourself first in your monthly budget. Make Savings a budget category like Phone and Electricity.

9) Invest the maximum allowed in your employer's tax deferred retirement plan.

10) Make extra principal payments in order to pay off your mortgage sooner.

STEP 3

Create Your Own Lifetime Investment Plan

How to put your prosperity dollars to work

There is a famous parable in the Bible about the wealthy man who gives three of his servants some money for safekeeping before he embarks on a long journey. He gives one servant five *talents*, or coins. He gives the second servant two talents, and to the third he gives only one.

The first servant doubles the number of talents he was given by "trading with them." The second servant also doubles his money through investments. And the third servant, obviously a well-meaning chap, takes the one talent his master had given him and buries it for safekeeping.

When the boss gets back, servant number one — the speculator — proudly shows his master how he had doubled his money. The master rewards him handsomely. Servant number two — the investor — was also rewarded for his efforts.

But servant number three — the saver — who proudly showed his master that he had succeeded in not losing the single talent entrusted to him, was cast aside "into the outer darkness."

The parable may have a separate theological theme, but its message is applicable here: It is wise to do more than just save your money. You must become an investor, or perhaps even a speculator if you want to be successful.

Saving a portion of what you earn is simply not enough. Government statistics show that between 1972 and 1987, the median income in this country rose 153 percent. Pretty healthy. But at the same time, inflation rose 170 percent, the average price of a home rose 294 percent, federal taxes for the average wage earner rose 175 percent, Social Security taxes rose 331 percent, and state and local taxes rose 520 percent! It is obvious that if you had simply saved your money during that time, expecting it to keep up with the cost of living, you no doubt would be cast aside into "the outer darkness" of poverty.

Study Table 3-1 a moment.

Table 3-1

WHAT HAPPENED TO $100		
	1/1/60	**1/1/90**
Small Company Stocks	$100	$6,199
Blue Chip Stocks	$100	$2,385
Short-Term T-bills	$100	$701
source: Ibbotson & Assoc. *Yearbook,* 1991		

It shows that if you had speculated with $100 in the stocks of rather small — and risky — companies back in 1960, by 1990 your $100 would be worth $6,199. If you had invested $100 in larger — and much more stable — blue chip companies, your $100 would have become $2,385 in 30 years.

But if you had parked your $100 in short-term treasury bills — which are very safe — you would only have $701 to show for it by 1990.

(There are obviously a number of variables I'm ignoring here, like changes in market conditions, commissions, and taxes. But the point is still valid.)

In order for you to achieve financial prosperity over a long period of time, you must do more than just save your *prosperity dollars*. You must invest some and even speculate with some.

What is the difference between speculating, investing, and saving?

"When speculators and investors get greedy, they ignore risk. When they are afraid, they are overwhelmed by risk."

RISK!

What Is Risk?

The *American Heritage Dictionary* defines risk as "The possibility of suffering harm or loss; danger."

You've probably heard that the two emotions that dictate investment decisions are greed and fear. When speculators and investors get greedy, they ignore risk. When they are afraid, they are overwhelmed by risk.

Good speculators and investors acknowledge and evaluate the level of risk in any investment and decide whether the risk is worth taking. There are four things that make an investment risky: volatility, liquidity, safety of principal, and intrinsic value.

Volatility: In the world of stocks and bonds, prices go up, and they go down. Sometimes they go up a lot, and sometimes they go down a lot. People who place a value judgment on price fluctuations (i.e., up is good and down is bad) do not understand the marketplace. When you invest money in stocks and bonds, there is always the risk that your investment will lose money. If you do, it does not mean you are a bad investor or that the system failed you. But a savvy investor understands the risk of price volatility *before* investing any money.

Generally speaking, stock issued by smaller companies will be rather volatile because the companies' earnings tend to fluctuate a lot. The stock prices of larger, more mature companies tend to be less volatile because their earnings are more predictable.

Liquidity: An investment is liquid if you are able to sell it easily without having to appreciably lower your asking price below current market levels. The stock market is generally liquid enough that you can easily sell shares at current market prices. The market for gold coins, though, is not as liquid. You often must reduce your asking price below market value in order to sell. The same is sometimes true of real estate, especially when undeveloped land is involved.

Safety of Principal: When you deposit money in a passbook savings account, your money is insured by the federal government. There is no risk involved because the bank can guarantee that you will get every penny back. But when you invest in the stock market, your money is not insured. There is absolutely no guarantee anywhere that you will get any of your principal investment back.

Intrinsic Value: Perhaps the most famous trading frenzy in history was the legendary "tulip mania" Holland experienced in the 1600s. Wealthy individuals imported rare bulbs into the country, and they began trading them at prices many times their intrinsic — or actual — value. Of course, the mania eventually ended, and hundreds of speculators lost quite a bit of money.

The lesson here is that the closer the amount you pay for an investment is to its actual value, the less risk is involved. The amount you pay in excess of an investment's actual value is called a *premium*. Premiums are usually created by excessive demand for an investment.

Figure 3-1

THE PYRAMID OF RISK

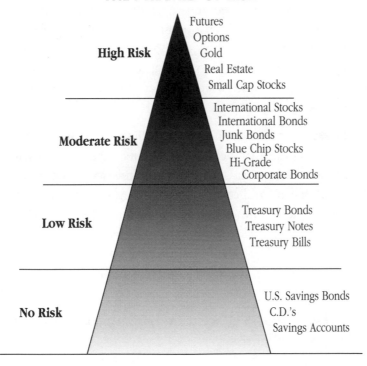

High Risk	Futures Options Gold Real Estate Small Cap Stocks
Moderate Risk	International Stocks International Bonds Junk Bonds Blue Chip Stocks Hi-Grade Corporate Bonds
Low Risk	Treasury Bonds Treasury Notes Treasury Bills
No Risk	U.S. Savings Bonds C.D.'s Savings Accounts

Figure 3-1 is a tool that financial planners use to show their clients how to construct a portfolio. The investments at the top of the pyramid are the riskiest, while those at the bottom are the safest.

The pyramid shape symbolizes the need to make safe investments the foundation of your portfolio. You can't build the top of the pyramid until the bottom is in place.

"A successful portfolio should include investments elected from every level of the risk pyramid"

A successful portfolio should include investments elected from every level of the risk pyramid, which means you should be a saver, an investor, and a speculator all at once.

Saver: A saver's objective is to preserve every penny by avoiding risk altogether. You should be a saver if you will soon be needing the money you are putting aside. People who, for example, are saving for a house they plan to buy in the near term should not put any of their down payment money at risk. Savers should concentrate on the lower third of the pyramid of risk.

Investor: Investors should be willing to assume some risk in order to achieve a higher return on their money than a saver gets. The key to success for investors is in allowing their money to grow over a long period of time. Generally speaking, the longer an investment is held, the greater the chance of a higher return. People in their 30s and 40s should be willing to take on a fair amount of risk with the money they are saving for retirement.

Investors should concentrate on the middle third of the pyramid of risk.

Speculator: Speculators actively seek out high-risk investments in order to make a short-term — and presumably lucrative — gain. Successful speculators will tell you that they also seek to control risk by quickly selling investments that do not perform up to their expectations. Another important key to success with speculations is in thoroughly understanding what you are investing in. Steer clear, for example, if your neighbor has a hot tip on a "can't miss" gold mining company that you've never heard of.

Speculators should concentrate on the upper third of the pyramid of risk.

Risk Tolerance Quiz

Here is a list of 10 questions that have little to do with the financial world, but have everything to do with the risks we are asked to take in everyday life. Some questions involve situations that are riskier than others. Answer each question honestly, and understand that there are no right or wrong answers. When you have answered all 10 questions, turn to pages 58–59 to see whether you are a speculator, an investor, or a saver.

Question #1: You and your date are in line to buy tickets for the 8:30 showing of the current #1 box office hit. The woman selling tickets informs you that the 8:30 show is sold out, but there are still tickets available for the midnight show. She then tells you there are seats available for an 8:45 sneak preview of a motion picture you have never heard of.

What would you do?

    A) Buy the sneak preview tickets.

    B) Wait for the midnight showing
       of the box office hit.

Question #2: During an appointment with your optometrist, she tells you about a new — and rather expensive — surgical procedure designed to correct vision problems like yours. If it was successful, you would no longer have to wear glasses. If it was not successful, you would still have to wear glasses. And there was a 20 percent chance that, even if the surgery was successful, your vision problem could return.

What would you do?

    A) Take a chance on the expensive surgical procedure.

    B) Buy another pair of glasses.

Question #3: A newly designed version of a hot sports car you have had your eye on for a long time is just released. It looks wonderful, and it drives beautifully, but the automotive press says it may have a few mechanical and electronic bugs that need to be worked out.

What would you do?

    A) Buy the car anyway.

    B) Wait for next year's model, and hope any potential bugs are worked out by then.

Question #4: The department store you are shopping in is having a close-out sale on sweaters. All sales are final. You find a style you love, but they don't have the color you want in your size. A clerk calls another store and discovers that it has the color and size you want. But, because it is a close-out sale, they will not hold it for you.

What would you do?

    A) Hurry to the other store, and hope the sweater is still available when you get there.

    B) Buy the sweater you have in your hand.

Question #5: You have just boarded a commercial airliner, and a flight attendant announces to all passengers that the flight has been overbooked. So they are offering a free ticket for a future flight to anyone who will give up their seat. The next scheduled flight to your destination is four hours later.

What would you do?

    A) Give up your seat and take the free ticket.

    B) Stay on your original flight.

Question #6: You are in an electronics store shopping for a new computer. After you decide on the model you want, the salesman offers you a choice: you can have the floor model at a 10 percent discount, or you can have a brand new model with no discount.

What would you do?

    A) Take the floor model and the discount.

    B) Take the new computer without the discount.

Question #7: It is summer vacation time. You decide to rent the same beach house you rented last year. It is located a few blocks from the shore, so it does not have a view of the ocean. Your travel agent tells you that another house located right on the water will be available a month later than you had planned to vacation. It is a wonderful house with a gorgeous view of the ocean. The only problem is it is only available during what is traditionally the stormy season.

What would you do?

    A) Take the house on the beach and hope it doesn't rain.

    B) Take the same house you rented the year before.

Question #8: You lose your job, and you spend the next year looking for another one. Finally, you are offered two different positions. One pays a lot more money than your previous job did, and it involves a lot of pressure and high-performance expectations. The other position pays less than your previous job did, but it offers a pleasant working atmosphere.

What would you do?

    A) Take the high-pressure, high-paying job.

    B) Take the low-pressure, low-paying job.

Question #9: You are preparing to board a 14-hour flight to Australia, and you have room in your travel bag for one book. You narrow it down to two choices: There is the latest novel of an author you have read before. But his last two books disappointed you. Or you can buy the current #1 bestseller that you know nothing about.

What would you do?

    A) Take the current bestseller.

    B) Take the book by the author you are familiar with.

Question #10: Your favorite baseball team makes it to the World Series. A close associate at work offers you a choice: You can attend game two with him tomorrow night, or you can wait to attend the much more exciting — and important — game seven. But, of course, there is no guarantee that there will be a game seven.

What would you do?

    A) Wait for the possible game seven.

    B) Go to game two.

Now turn to pages 58–59 to find out whether you are a saver, an investor, or a speculator. Knowing what your risk tolerance level is will help you put together your lifetime investment plan. (Later in the chapter, I have outlined suggested lifetime investment plans for all three categories.)

How to Invest for Your Retirement

Instead of *saving* for retirement, you should *invest* for retirement. Inflation, no matter how low it is, still eats up most, if not all, of a saver's gains over the years. It's like burying your money in the ground. You should also be an investor your whole life. The only way a retired person on a fixed income keeps up with inflation is to have a portion of his or her nest egg invested at all times. If you don't, you're making the mistake of investing on the market's terms.

Investing on the Market's Terms

In 1991, a few well-known investment advisors told their newsletter subscribers to take their money out of stocks and bonds and put it into Treasury bills. Their indicators told them that the markets were too risky to stay in, and they were afraid a major price decline was coming.

Over the next two years, they missed the most dramatic bond rally in a generation that brought interest rates down to 30-year lows, and they missed 1,000 points on the Dow Jones Industrial Average. They were investing on the market's terms.

What I mean is they decided when to get in and out of the markets by using all the mathematical and statistical tools used by savvy money managers: P/E ratios, book value, dividend yield, market momentum, and market sentiment. And it is true that, on a historical basis, these market indicators showed that stock and bond prices were generally too high for their own good in 1991.

But prices continued to rise in 1992 and 1993. And my friends the investment advisors who based their investment decisions on market signals didn't participate in those market increases. No, they didn't lose any money. But they didn't make nearly as much as they could have if they had only invested on their own terms.

Investing on Your Terms

Instead of trying to beat the market by guessing when a major top or bottom is coming, play the game on your terms. Invest based on five very personal criteria:

Your Needs. Before you ever invest a dime, you should know *why* you are investing, whether it is for retirement, your child's college education, to accumulate the down payment for a new home, or whatever. That will help you determine how much money you need to invest and how much risk you can tolerate.

Your Expectations. Decide ahead of time how you expect a particular investment to perform. When risk is involved, you should understand that you could lose money. But you should also expect to make more over time than you would from a passbook savings account.

Your Time Horizon. As I said before, your personal time horizon dictates how much risk you should be willing to assume. When you are young, you can afford to take risks. So financial planners suggest you lean toward more aggressive investments that — given enough time — may provide a greater return than more conservative investments.

If you are close to retirement age, or if your child is close to college age, you should reduce the amount of risk you are exposed to.

Your Risk Tolerance. How did you score on the Risk Tolerance Quiz earlier in the chapter? That will help determine how you allocate the assets in your portfolio. It is one thing to say that it is good to assume a lot of risk when you are young. But the fact is you should be comfortable with the amount of risk in your portfolio. And if you aren't able to sleep at night because you're worrying about losing money, you shouldn't be in too many risky investments.

Your Knowledge of the Investment. Never invest in something you're not familiar with. Don't let brokers, neighbors, and relatives talk you into an investment you don't fully understand.

Your Lifetime Investment Plan

An investment plan should last a lifetime. And depending on your needs, expectations, time horizon, risk tolerance, and level of understanding of what you're investing in, you should be exposed to all levels of risk, in varying degrees, at all times.

To simplify things, I have identified three distinct levels of investment risk, and I have labeled them with traditional investment objectives used by many mutual funds.

Aggressive Growth: These are the riskiest investments in your portfolio. They include gold mining companies, small companies with the potential to grow faster than the whole economy, companies in foreign countries with the potential for rapid growth, and high yielding corporate bonds issued by companies with debt ratings below "investment" grade (better known as "junk" bonds).

"You and/or your financial planner really need to complete your personal lifetime investment plan."

Growth & Income: These investments carry risk, but they are more stable in their growth patterns and less volatile in their price fluctuations. They include mature, blue chip companies that tend to grow at the same rate the whole economy does, investment grade corporate bonds, and long-term Treasury bonds.

Capital Preservation: These investments carry little or no risk. They include short- to intermediate-term Treasury bills and notes, and money market mutual funds.

Using these three investment categories, here is an outline of three *suggested* lifetime investment plans:

- *One for a speculator*, who fully understands, and is comfortable with, risk.

- *One for an investor*, who also understands risk, but is not as comfortable with it as the speculator is.

- *And one for the saver*, who understands risk, but tries to avoid it.

I have included *suggested* allocations based on at least two factors: your age and your risk tolerance level. But keep in mind it does not take into account your very personal needs at any given moment, nor the expectations you may have of your portfolio. So you and/or your financial planner really need to complete your personal lifetime investment plan.

But Figure 3-2 is a start.

Figure 3-2

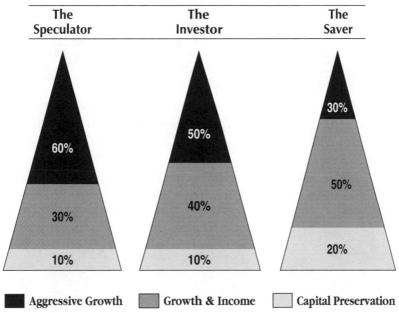

AGES 25–40

The Speculator	The Investor	The Saver

Aggressive Growth   Growth & Income   Capital Preservation

Because you are still more than 20 years away from retirement, clearly half of your portfolio is in riskier investments that you hope will provide a decent return.

The Growth & Income category should be the core of your portfolio. Therefore, it should remain the same. Only the Aggressive Growth and Capital Preservation categories change as you age.

Any dividends you earn at this point should be automatically reinvested so that your growth rate is compounded. (At the end of the chapter, I have an exercise designed to illustrate the magic of compound growth.)

At this stage of your life, the amount invested in Capital Preservation should be earmarked for emergencies and opportunities that may come up.

Figure 3-3

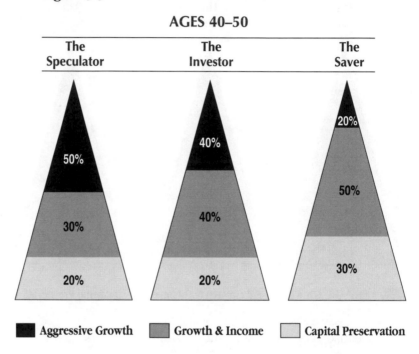

AGES 40–50

The Speculator	The Investor	The Saver

Aggressive Growth   Growth & Income   Capital Preservation

When you hit age 40 (Figure 3-3), start thinking about reducing some of the risk in your portfolio by transferring a portion of your investments from Aggressive Growth to Capital Appreciation. Don't change your allocation to Growth & Income and continue to re-invest any dividends.

Note: I do not mean to imply that you should not continue to buy and sell what you hold in the *Growth & Income* category. I'm only talking about maintaining a constant percentage of your portfolio in the category.

Figure 3-4

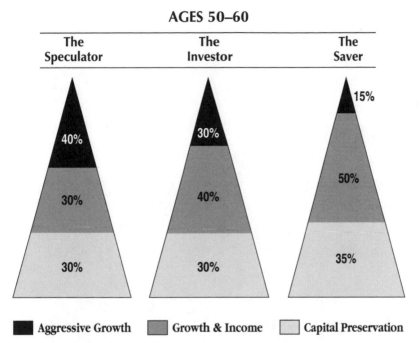

AGES 50–60

The Speculator	The Investor	The Saver
40%	30%	15%
30%	40%	50%
30%	30%	35%

■ Aggressive Growth ▨ Growth & Income ▢ Capital Preservation

Continue to rotate a portion of your portfolio out of Aggressive Growth and into Capital Preservation. (Figure 3-4)

Note: Are you planning to retire at age 55? (Aren't we all?) If you are, you might consider skipping to the allocations suggested for the 60–70 age group (which is designed to maximize income and minimize risk), especially if you aren't planning to draw Social Security until your full retirement age, which could be as much as 12 years later! (Figure 3-5)

Figure 3-5

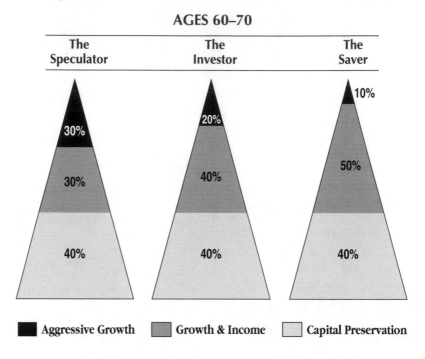

AGES 60–70

The Speculator	The Investor	The Saver

Aggressive Growth   Growth & Income   Capital Preservation

It is during this period that you will probably retire and start to draw income from your portfolio. Hopefully, you won't have to withdraw any of the principal, and you can live on the interest income your portfolio produces. That will obviously depend on the other sources of retirement income you have, such as Social Security or a corporate pension.

Figure 3-6

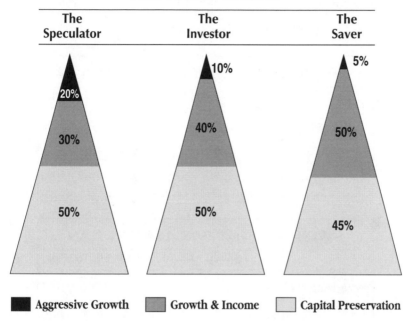

AGE 70 AND BEYOND

The Speculator	The Investor	The Saver

Aggressive Growth   Growth & Income   Capital Preservation

After I outlined my plan to one of the many investment seminars I speak at each year, a gentleman in the audience stood up, announced to the gathering that he was in his mid-70s, and thanked me for still considering him an investor.

Yes, even after age 70, you should still be an investor. Expecting your retirement nest egg to keep up with inflation when all of it is in safe, low-yielding investments such as Treasury bills and certificates of deposit is unreasonable.

Table 3-2 is a quick outline of the suggested lifetime investment plans for the speculator, the investor, and the saver.

Table 3-2: Lifetime Investment Plans

SPECULATOR'S LIFETIME INVESTMENT PLAN				
25–40	40–50	50–60	60–70	70–
Aggressive Growth: 60%	50%	40%	30%	20%
Growth & Income: 30%	30%	30%	30%	30%
Capital Preservation: 10%	20%	30%	40%	50%

INVESTOR'S LIFETIME INVESTMENT PLAN				
25–40	40–50	50–60	60–70	70–
Aggressive Growth: 50%	40%	30%	20%	10%
Growth & Income: 40%	40%	40%	40%	40%
Capital Preservation: 10%	20%	30%	40%	50%

SAVER'S LIFETIME INVESTMENT PLAN				
25–40	40–50	50–60	60–70	70–
Aggressive Growth: 30%	20%	15%	10%	5%
Growth & Income: 50%	50%	50%	50%	50%
Capital Preservation: 20%	30%	35%	40%	45%

Footnote: The Magic of Compounding

Earlier, I mentioned the importance of re-investing dividends in order to maximize the compound growth rate of your portfolio. Here is a quick exercise that illustrates the magic of compounding:

Let's assume you land a temporary, freelance job that will last 30 working days, and you are given the option of choosing how you will be paid.

If you chose the first option, you would be paid $1,000 a day.

If you chose the second option, you would be paid a penny the first day, two cents the next day, and then a doubling of the previous day's total thereafter. (i.e., four cents the next day, eight cents the next day, sixteen cents the next day, etc.)

If you chose the first payment option, it is pretty clear that you would have earned $30,000.

But if you chose the second option, you would have been paid a total of $10,737,418.23. (Don't believe it? I have the whole calculation illustrated on the next page.) That is the magic of compounding. Re-investing dividends and interest is one of the easiest, fastest, most dependable ways of letting your portfolio grow over time.

How the "Magic of Compounding" Story Was Computed

If you selected the first payment option ($1,000 a day for 30 days) here is how you would have been paid:

	Payment	Cumulative Total
Day 1:	$1,000	$1,000
Day 2:	$1,000	$2,000
Day 3:	$1,000	$3,000
Day 4:	$1,000	$4,000
Day 5:	$1,000	$5,000
Day 6:	$1,000	$6,000
Day 7:	$1,000	$7,000
Day 8:	$1,000	$8,000
Day 9:	$1,000	$9,000
Day 10:	$1,000	$10,000
Day 11:	$1,000	$11,000
Day 12:	$1,000	$12,000
Day 13:	$1,000	$13,000
Day 14:	$1,000	$14,000
Day 15:	$1,000	$15,000
Day 16:	$1,000	$16,000
Day 17:	$1,000	$17,000
Day 18:	$1,000	$18,000
Day 19:	$1,000	$19,000
Day 20:	$1,000	$20,000
Day 21:	$1,000	$21,000
Day 22:	$1,000	$22,000
Day 23:	$1,000	$23,000
Day 24:	$1,000	$24,000
Day 25:	$1,000	$25,000
Day 26:	$1,000	$26,000
Day 27:	$1,000	$27,000
Day 28:	$1,000	$28,000
Day 29:	$1,000	$29,000
Day 30:	$1,000	$30,000

If you chose the second method of payment (a penny the first day, and a doubling of the previous day's total thereafter), here is how you would have been paid:

	Payment	Cumulative Total
Day 1:	$.01	$.01
Day 2:	$.02	$.03
Day 3:	$.04	$.07
Day 4:	$.08	$.15
Day 5:	$.16	$.31
Day 6:	$.32	$.63
Day 7:	$.64	$1.27
Day 8:	$1.28	$2.55
Day 9:	$2.56	$5.11
Day 10:	$5.12	$10.23
Day 11:	$10.24	$20.47
Day 12:	$20.48	$40.95
Day 13:	$40.96	$81.91
Day 14:	$81.92	$163.83
Day 15:	$163.84	$327.67
Day 16:	$327.68	$655.35
Day 17:	$655.36	$1,310.71
Day 18:	$1,310.72	$2,621.43
Day 19:	$2,621.44	$5,242.87
Day 20:	$5,242.88	$10,485.75
Day 21:	$10,485.76	$20,971.51
Day 22:	$20,971.52	$41,943.03
Day 23:	$41,943.04	$83,886.07
Day 24:	$83,886.08	$167,772.15
Day 25:	$167,772.16	$335,544.31
Day 26:	$335,544.32	$671,088.63
Day 27:	$671,088.64	$1,342,177.27
Day 28:	$1,342,177.28	$2,684,354.55
Day 29:	$2,684,354.56	$5,368,709.11
Day 30:	$5,368,709.12	$10,737,418.23

Risk Tolerance Quiz Results

Remember, there are no right and wrong answers to this quiz. Each question provided two choices. One choice was always riskier than the other. And the level of risk varied from question to question. (Question #2 about the eye surgery, for example, involved more risk than question #1 about choosing which movie to see.)

I divided the questions into three categories:

- *High risk*
- *Moderate risk*
- *Low risk*

I assigned a point weighting to each question, based on its level of risk. In every case, response A was the riskier choice in each question. So give yourself the points assigned for every question where you chose response A.

	Risk Points	**Your Points**
1)	1	_____
2)	10	_____
3)	5	_____
4)	1	_____
5)	1	_____
6)	5	_____
7)	5	_____
8)	10	_____
9)	1	_____
10)	1	_____
	Total Points	_____

There are 40 possible points. In other words, if you took the riskier route in each question, you will score a total of 40 points.

How did you do? I have divided possible point totals into three categories.

Total Points	Category
25–40	Speculator
10–25	Investor
0–10	Saver

By the way, I scored a 13, which makes me an *investor*. (I didn't choose the high-pressure job or the eye surgery. But I did buy the sports car right away!)

STEP 4

Let Mutual Funds Be Your Vehicle to Prosperity

Everything you need to know about
"the perfect investment"

In the fall of 1992, CNBC asked me to co-host a half-hour program in prime time about mutual funds with famed Wall Street investor Jim Rogers. Jimmy made a mint in the '70s managing the Quantum Fund with legendary speculator George Soros. He retired at the age of 37 in 1980. (I'm 37 as I write this, and unless this book sells a zillion copies, I won't be retiring next year. Or next decade, for that matter. I hate this guy.)

"Your Portfolio" debuted in October 1992, and right away the ratings were very strong. Mutual funds are very very popular. Right now, there is more money invested in mutual funds than there is deposited in government-insured deposit accounts.

And for good reason: A mutual fund is the perfect investment. I don't just mean that mutual funds are the perfect investment for the '90s, or for people saving for retirement or college. I mean: A mutual fund is the perfect investment. Period.

Now let me be perfectly clear about this. I am *not* suggesting that all mutual funds are created equal. Some are certainly better than others. Much better.

My point is that the *concept* of a mutual fund is perfect for virtually every investment need.

As I said in Chapter 3, it is not enough anymore just to save your money. You must invest it. And for my money, the best way to invest it is through a mutual fund.

What Is a Mutual Fund?

A mutual fund is a company that pools money from hundreds, or thousands, of investors who have similar investment objectives, and invests the money in a variety of things.

Some funds invest only in stocks, some only in bonds, and some invest in stocks and bonds. Some invest in real estate. Some invest in Ginnie Maes.

Some funds are very risky by design, while some are very conservative. Some provide investors with taxable income, while others provide tax-exempt income.

Advantages

- *Mutual funds give you instant diversification.* If the value of some of the stocks or bonds in your mutual fund decline on a given day, chances are the value of some others will appreciate.

- *Your money is managed by professionals.* They have access to huge databases of information about stocks, bonds, or whatever they are investing in. And often they will visit companies and talk with chief executives to find out how business is before they invest. In other words, they do all the homework that should be done before you invest.

Disadvantages

- *People rarely get rich investing in mutual funds.* (Jimmy Rogers is an exception.) Funds are generally designed to provide investors with a slow, steady increase in the value of their money through diversification. And while diversification generally reduces risk, it also tempers returns.

- *A number of fees and hidden charges imposed by some mutual funds can eat away at your profits.* The solution is to know what those charges are before you invest, and to invest in a fund over a long period of time in order to minimize the impact of those charges.

A Quick History of Mutual Funds

Conventional wisdom has it that the first mutual funds were created roughly 200 years ago in Europe. They first played a role in American history when some of these European funds, or trusts as they are called over there, invested in rebuilding a number of U.S. cities after the Civil War.

"In 1940, there was $448 million dollars invested in mutual funds. Today, there is more than $2 trillion in them, and the number of funds available now exceeds the number of stocks traded on the New York Stock Exchange."

The first American mutual fund was created in Boston in 1924 to help small investors participate in the stock market boom at that time. Now mutual funds are experiencing their own boom. In 1940, there was $448 million dollars invested in mutual funds. Today, there is more than *$2 trillion* in them, and the number of funds available now exceeds the number of stocks traded on the New York Stock Exchange.

Mutual fund companies are regulated by the Securities and Exchange Commission, just as brokerage houses are. And the regulations governing mutual funds are changing all the time. For years after the Great Depression of the 1930s, commercial banks were not allowed to be direct players in the investment world. The Glass-Steagall Act prohibited them from using depositors' money for anything riskier than loans to businesses.

But now that the financial services business has been deregulated by the government, banks want to participate in the securities business again. And, slowly but surely, they are being allowed to. Some banks are now able to offer their customers a choice of depositing their money in a savings account, parking it in a certificate of deposit, or investing it in a mutual fund.

But the trend has not been completely without controversy. A survey released by the SEC in the fall of 1993 found that a number of customers who purchased shares in mutual funds through their banks thought they were insured by the government the way passbook savings accounts are. They most certainly are not.

Open-End and Closed-End Funds

There are two broad categories of mutual funds: open end and closed end.

Open-End Funds

This type of fund has an open-ended number of shares. When you invest, the investment company essentially creates the shares for you. When you sell them back — or *redeem* them, in mutual fund language — the shares cease to exist.

This is important, because at the end of each trading day, an investment company will determine what each share of a mutual fund is worth by adding up the value of its portfolio and dividing that by the number of mutual fund shares outstanding. The result is its net asset value, or NAV.

Some very successful mutual funds have stopped taking money from new investors, funds like the Acorn Fund, managed by Ralph Wanger in Chicago; or the CGM Capital Development Fund, managed by Kenneth Heebner in Boston; or the Sequoia Fund, managed by Bill Ruane and Rick Cunniff in New York. These funds became very popular with investors because of their strong performances over a number of years. But their managers found it impossible to keep up with all the new money coming in.

Closed-End Funds

These funds issue a finite number of shares to the public, and then those shares trade on stock exchanges just like stocks. The most prominent examples of closed-end funds are the funds that invest in stocks in foreign countries — the so-called closed-end country funds. In 1983, there were only three closed-end country funds. Today there are more than 40.

Investors need to be very aware of how closed-end funds are priced. A fund's shares will trade at either a *premium* or a *discount* relative to its net asset value. For example, if a closed-end fund's net asset value (or the actual value of its holdings) is $5.00 a share and the fund's shares are trading on the exchange at $5.50, then any investor buying shares today would be paying 10 percent more than the fund's actual value. In other words, they would be paying a 10 percent premium.

Conversely, if the same fund's shares were trading on the exchange at $4.50 a share, a new investor would be paying 10 percent less than the fund's actual value. They would be getting a 10 percent discount.

Savvy investors try never to pay a premium for the shares of a closed-end mutual fund.

The premiums and discounts of all closed-end funds are listed once a week in *Barron's* and in the business sections of various newspapers around the country.

Mutual Fund Fees

When you buy or sell a stock or bond, you pay your broker a commission for the time spent executing the order. A pretty straightforward process.

It's not that simple with mutual funds. Some mutual funds charge a fee when you buy shares; some charge when you sell your shares. Others don't charge you a fee when you buy or sell, but they charge you for other things.

Before you buy shares in any mutual fund, find out how much of a fee you will have to pay and when you will have to pay it.

What follows are descriptions of the typical mutual fund fees you should know about.

Front-End Load

In mutual fund language, the fee you pay a mutual fund company is called a "load." You pay a front-end load when you *buy* shares in a fund. Fund families typically charge front-end loads when they market their funds through broker dealers. For example, you cannot buy shares in Putnam mutual funds directly from Putnam. You must buy them through brokers licensed by Putnam. And when you buy, you pay the broker. The broker then keeps you informed about how your fund is performing, and he or she is free to make recommendations to you about what to do with your investments.

Loads can be anywhere from 1.5 percent to 8.5 percent of your initial investment. So for example, if the load on a fund you purchase is 5 percent, the broker charges $5 for every $100 you invest.

Back-End Load

This is sometimes also referred to as a *Contingent Deferred Sales Charge (CDSC)*. You are charged a back-end load when you sell your shares. Some funds charge a flat fee. Others have begun implementing these contingent deferred sales charges where the fee you are charged is based on how long you held your shares.

For example, with some CDSCs, you are charged, say, 3 percent if you only hold your shares one year. You are charged 2 percent if you hold them at least two years. You are charged 1 percent if you hold them at least three years, and you are not charged anything if you hold the shares longer than three years.

Some funds are now issuing Class A shares and Class B shares in the same fund. Class A shares typically charge a front-end load, while Class B shares offer a contingency deferred sales charge.

Class B shares would appear to be the better deal if you planned to hold shares in a mutual fund for a long time. But you should be aware that if you own Class B shares in a fund, you are usually charged a 12(b)-1 fee.

12b-1 Fee

This is a rather controversial mutual fund fee that was created in 1980. Its name comes from its designation in the Securities and Exchange Commission rules.

"And unlike load funds, where brokers continue to offer money management advice, no-load funds generally don't come with such advice."

Mutual funds are permitted to charge investors a 12b-1 fee in order to pay broker commissions or for things like advertising costs. In 1993, a cap was placed on all 12b-1 fees. Funds cannot charge investors more than .75 percent of a fund's assets on an annual basis.

Critics of 12b-1 fees charge that they are unnecessary and excessive. Proponents say the money used to advertise the fund enhances the fund's value by bringing in more shareholders.

As an investor, you should be aware when a fund charges a 12b-1 fee, how much it is, and what the money is used for. Fund companies must outline such information in their prospectuses.

No-Load Funds

Some funds don't charge you anything when you buy or sell shares. These are called no-load funds. You purchase shares directly from the mutual fund company. But you're not getting something for free. With no-load funds, you periodically pay a small *management fee.*

And unlike load funds, where brokers continue to offer money management advice, no-load funds generally don't come with such advice. The operators you deal with at no-load mutual fund companies are there to take your orders and to answer questions about how a particular fund works or what it invests in. But they are not qualified to offer advice.

How to Buy Shares in Mutual Funds

There are essentially two ways to purchase shares in a mutual fund.

- *Directly from the investment company.* This is the way you can buy shares in open-end mutual funds that do not charge a load up front. You call the investment company directly, and they send you a prospectus for their funds and an application. The investment company will then periodically send you information about your fund's performance.

  A number of large investment companies offer convenient services that allow you to invest new money in their funds via electronic deductions from your bank account, and you can switch money from one fund to another within the same investment company over the telephone.

- *Through a broker.* This is how you purchase shares in open-end mutual funds that charge a front-end load. And this is how you purchase shares in closed-end funds that trade on stock exchanges. And some large discount brokerage companies like Charles Schwab and Jack White now allow their customers to purchase shares in a number of load and no-load funds.

Mutual Fund Categories

The larger investment companies offer a full menu of mutual funds with a broad range of investment objectives. They are listed below in alphabetical order.

Aggressive Growth

As the name implies, these funds are aggressive in their approach to investing. Their objective is to make as much money as possible, and they are not afraid to assume some risk in order to accomplish the goal. Typically, these funds invest in smaller companies with the greatest growth potential, or in large out-of-favor companies that may be ready to rebound.

Balanced

Most mutual funds either try to provide their shareholders with a monthly dividend, or they try simply to make as much money as they can (in mutual fund language that is called "achieving capital appreciation"). Balanced funds try to do both by putting together a balanced portfolio of stocks and bonds in order to achieve three investment objectives simultaneously:

1) Protecting investors' principal.

2) Paying current income.

3) Achieving long-term growth.

Balanced funds are designed to be relatively safe. But you should be aware that they traditionally don't pay as much income as a traditional income fund, and they don't make as much money as a traditional growth fund.

Corporate Bond

These funds are designed to provide shareholders with a relatively high level of income. Most of their portfolios are made up of bonds issued by corporations. Corporate bonds are riskier than Treasury bonds, and they yield more. These funds also devote a portion of their portfolios to safer Treasury bonds and to bonds issued by federal agencies like Federal National Mortgage Association (Fannie Mae) and Government National Mortgage Association (Ginnie Mae).

Flexible Portfolio

When you buy shares in a stock fund, the fund manager is obligated to keep your money invested in stocks, no matter what condition the stock market is in. The story is the same with bond funds. But it is a different story with flexible funds. They allow fund managers to move money to where the greatest opportunities are. During one period, your fund may look like a bond fund, during another it may look like a stock fund, or it may hold a lot of so-called cash instruments if neither stocks nor bonds look good. Depending on the fund manager, this flexibility could result in a high turnover rate (meaning the manager does a lot of short-term trading), and that could mean a relatively high tax bite for shareholders.

"During one period, your fund may look like a bond fund, during another it may look like a stock fund, or it may hold a lot of so-called cash instruments if neither stocks nor bonds look good."

Ginnie Mae

These funds invest in so-called mortgage backed securities issued by the federal agency known as Government National Mortgage Association, or Ginnie Mae. Investors looking for monthly income will typically look to Ginnie Mae funds for some of that income.

Global Bond

These funds invest in corporate and Treasury bonds in the United States and anywhere else in the world. Some global bond funds look for the highest yield (meaning higher risk), some look for higher quality (and lower risk), and some look for a combination of the two. As with any fund that invests internationally, there is a currency risk. That means if the value of the currency of the country you're invested in declines, the value of your holdings will, too. (Unless the fund manager successfully hedges against currency fluctuations. Some are allowed to and some are not, because hedging involves trading in risky, and expensive, futures contracts.)

Global Equity

Same story as global bond funds. Global equity funds invest in stocks in the United States and anywhere else in the world.

Growth

These funds typically invest in established blue chip companies. Their aim is to make money (to achieve capital gains). They normally do not pay any dividend income.

Growth and Income

These are the "have-your-cake-and-eat-it-too" mutual funds. The stocks they invest in are expected to show a steady increase in share price *and* pay a steady stream of dividend income.

High-Yield Bond

These funds invest in what are endearingly known as junk bonds. They are issued by corporations that aren't exactly in perfect financial condition, so credit rating services like Standard & Poor's or Moody's give them what are called "below investment grade" ratings. Hence, the name "junk." The good news for investors is that junk bonds provide above-average yields. The bad news is they also carry above-average risk.

Income-Bond

These funds invest in a combination of government and corporate bonds. Their aim is to provide shareholders with a steady stream of income.

Income-Equity
These funds also aim to provide shareholders with a steady stream of income, and they do it by investing in stocks with a good track record of paying dividends.

Income-Mixed
These funds provide income to shareholders by investing in a combination of government and corporate bonds and dividend-paying stocks.

Index
Virtually all mutual fund managers who invest in the stock market have one performance goal in mind: to beat the overall stock market. They will often say to themselves, "If my fund can do better than the Standard & Poor's 500 Index over a certain period of time, then I have done my job." But the fact is that, over a long period of time, most equity mutual funds do *not* perform better than the overall market. So someone came up with the idea of developing mutual funds that only invest in stocks that make up indices like the S&P 500. That way you're not competing with the market, you're investing in it. Obviously, index funds do well when the overall market is rising, and they do poorly when the market is going down. So shareholders must exercise patience and take a long-term view when investing in index funds.

"But the fact is that, over a long period of time, most equity mutual funds do not perform better than the overall market."

International
I mentioned global funds before, which may invest in any country in the world including the United States. International funds, in contrast, may invest in any country in the world *except* the United States. These funds got hot in the early '90s as individual investors discovered the rapidly growing economies in Asia

and Latin America. There are tremendous growth opportunities around the world as small, developing countries emerge into the free market. But there can also be tremendous risks involved. Besides the currency fluctuations U.S. investors must contend with, there are also political considerations.

Long-Term Municipal Bond

These funds invest in bonds issued by states and municipalities to finance the construction of airports, highways, bridges, schools, hospitals, and other public projects. Munis, as they are known, are popular with investors because in most cases the income derived is not taxed by the federal government. Some are also not taxed by state and local governments. (They are the so-called "triple tax-free munis.") These are popular with people who earn a high income, but they are definitely not restricted to those individuals.

And don't forget, while any *income* you receive from a municipal bond or bond fund may be tax exempt, when you sell your holdings any *profit* or *capital gains* you receive is taxable.

Money Market

These funds invest in short-term securities like Treasury bills, certificates of deposit of large banks, and short-term debt issued by large corporations (also known as "commercial paper"). These funds typically provide a yield slightly higher than a passbook savings account offers. And some mutual fund groups offer money market funds with check writing privileges. But if they do, make sure the price of the money market fund does not *fluctuate.* If it does, and you write checks against the fund as the fund's price is rising, you will have to pay capital gains taxes on each check you write. So make sure the money market fund maintains a single price of, say, $1.00 before you take advantage of any check writing capabilities.

Precious Metals/Gold

These funds invest at least two-thirds of their portfolio in companies that mine for gold, silver, or other precious metals. They also invest in the precious metals themselves. Obviously, these funds will do well when precious metals prices are rising, and they do not do well when prices are falling.

Sector

Sector funds invest in companies in a single industry group. There are utilities funds, for example, that invest only in public utilities. Other sector funds include technology funds, energy funds, and financial services funds, to name a few. These funds tend to be more volatile, and therefore riskier, than more broadly based mutual funds because they are not as diversified.

State Municipal Bond

These funds invest in municipal bonds issued in a single state. They provide investors who live in that state an exemption from federal *and* state taxes on the income earned by the fund.

United States Government Income

These funds invest in a variety of government securities, including Treasury bonds and mortgage-backed securities. It is important to note that while these funds invest in federally guaranteed securities, the funds themselves are *not* guaranteed the way a passbook savings account at a bank is.

Mutual Funds and Taxes

It is important to note that the IRS allows investment companies to pass on their investment-related tax liabilities to their shareholders.

Each year, usually in December, a fund announces how much it intends to pay its shareholders, either in the form of income or a capital gain.

If the fund pays its shareholders a capital gain, the shareholders are liable for the 28 percent capital gains tax. Shareholders are taxed at their own individual tax rate for any income a fund pays.

Investors do not pay taxes on the income paid by tax-exempt municipal bond funds, but they must pay capital gains taxes when they sell shares in muni bond funds.

Note: If you ever find yourself ready to invest in a mutual fund in December, find out whether the fund has declared its shareholder payout for the year. Then invest *after* the payout has been made. Otherwise, you will end up paying taxes on money you just invested.

How to Find a Mutual Fund That Meets Your Investment Needs

Before you invest in any mutual fund, you must ask yourself two key questions:

1) Why am I investing? Are you saving money for retirement, your child's college education, a new house, or what? Knowing what the money will eventually be used for helps determine which mutual fund to invest in.

2) When will I need the money? Generally speaking, the longer your time horizon is, the more risk you will be able to take. Because — again, generally speaking — the mutual funds that take on the most risk provide better returns *over longer periods of time.*

For example, if you are saving money to buy a house in, say, two to five years, you probably would not want to invest in a risky aggressive growth fund. A more conservative balanced fund might be a better idea. On the other hand, if you are saving for a retirement that won't begin for 10 to 20 years, an aggressive growth fund might provide you a larger nest egg than a balanced fund would.

"If you are saving for a retirement that won't begin for 10 to 20 years, an aggressive growth fund might provide you a larger nest egg than a balanced fund would."

For More Information about Mutual Funds

There are a number of services that track mutual fund performance. But the two largest, and best known, are Morningstar and Lipper Analytical Services. Most public libraries carry their materials, or you can write or call them directly to subscribe.

Morningstar
225 W. Wacker Dr.
Chicago, IL 60606
(800) 876–5005

Lipper Analytical Services
74 Trinity Pl.
New York, NY 10006
(212) 393–1300

For information specifically about closed-end mutual funds, probably the best known service is Thomas J. Herzfeld Advisors.

Thomas J. Herzfeld Advisors
P.O. Box 161465
Miami, FL 33116
(305) 271–1900

For beginners, the Mutual Fund Education Alliance publishes a 40-page booklet called "Directing Your Own Mutual Fund Investments," plus a 60-minute audio tape designed to help individuals understand how mutual funds work.

> *Mutual Fund Education Alliance*
> 1900 Erie St. Suite 120
> Kansas City, MO 64116
> (816) 471–1454

And the Investment Company Institute also publishes a number of pamphlets for beginners.

> *Investment Company Institute*
> P.O. Box 66140
> Washington, DC 20035–6140
> (202) 293–7700

Mutual Fund Families

I'm not going to recommend a particular family of funds to you. Rather, I have listed 40 of the largest and best known fund families around the country.

Call a few of them; ask for their introductory brochures. See what kinds of funds they offer, and which ones may meet your specific needs.

(**Note:** There are hundreds of other fund families that offer fine products. I'm not suggesting that you confine yourself to the 40 families listed here. But this is a start.)

1) *Aetna Mutual Funds*
   Hartford, CT
   (800) 238–6263

2) *The Benham Group*
   Mountain View, CA
   (800) 472–3389

3) *Berger Associates, Inc.*
Denver, CO
(800) 333–1001

4) *The Boston Company*
Boston, MA
(800) 225–5267

5) *Bull & Bear Group*
New York, NY
(800) 847–4200

6) *CGM Funds*
Boston, MA
(800) 345–4048

7) *Dreyfus Corporation*
Uniondale, NY
(800) 782–6620
Ext. 4025

8) *Fidelity Investments*
Boston, MA
(800) 544–8888

9) *Founders Funds*
Denver, CO
(800) 525–2440

10) *FundTrust Funds*
New York, NY
(800) 638–1896

11) *Gabelli Funds*
Rye, NY
(800) 422–3554

12) *G.T. Global
Growth Funds*
San Francisco, CA
(800) 824–1580

13) *John Hancock Group
of Funds*
Boston, MA
(800) 225–5291

14) *INVESCO Funds
Group*
Denver, CO
(800) 525–8085

15) *Janus Capital
Corporation*
Denver, CO
(800) 525–8983

16) *Jones & Babson, Inc.*
Kansas City, MO
(800) 422–2766

17) *The Kaufmann
Fund, Inc.*
New York, NY
(800) 666–6151

18) *Lexington Group of
Investment Companies*
Saddle Brook, NJ
(800) 526–0057

19) *Loomis Sayles Funds*
Boston, MA
(800) 633–3330

20) *Morgan Stanley Funds*
Boston, MA
(800) 548–7786

21) *Neuberger and Berman Funds*
New York, NY
(800) 877–9700

22) *Nuveen Mutual Funds*
Chicago, IL
(800) 257–8787

23) *The Oakmark Funds*
Chicago, IL
(800) 476–9625

24) *Pioneer Funds*
Boston, MA
(800) 225–6292

25) *Putnam Group of Mutual Funds*
Boston, MA
(800) 225–2465

26) *SAFECO Mutual Funds*
Seattle, WA
(800) 426–6730

27) *Charles Schwab Funds*
San Francisco, CA
(800) 526–8600

28) *Scudder Stevens & Clark, Inc.*
Boston, MA
(800) 225–2470

29) *State Street Funds*
Boston, MA
(800) 562–0032

30) *SteinRoe & Farnham Funds*
Chicago, IL
(800) 338–2550

31) *Strong Funds*
Milwaukee, WI
(800) 368–1030

32) *Templeton Group of Funds*
St. Petersburg, FL
(800) 237–0738

33) *T. Rowe Price Associates, Inc.*
Baltimore, MD
(800) 638–5660

34) *Twentieth Century Mutual Funds*
Kansas City, MO
(800) 345–2021

35) *United Services Advisors, Inc.*
San Antonio, TX
(800) 873–8637

36) *USAA Investment Management Co.*
San Antonio, TX
(800) 382–USAA

37) *Van Eck Funds*
New York, NY
(800) 221–2220

38) *Vanguard Group*
Valley Forge, PA
(800) 523–0857

39) *Van Kampen Merritt Funds*
Oakbrook Terrace, IL
(800) 225–2222

40) *Zweig Series Trust*
New York, NY
(800) 272–2700

STEP 5

Manage Your Debt
*How to turn Deficit Dollars
into Prosperity Dollars*

I got my first credit card during my junior year in college. It came with the checking account I opened at the local bank branch near campus.

Two important things happened to me at the same time: I got my first job in television, hosting a weekly news program for a local PBS affiliate in Los Angeles, and I got married. So I quit school, figuring I didn't need it anymore. After all, I already had a good job, a wife...and a credit card. I was Mr. Big Shot.

The credit limit on the card was something like $500. I hit that in no time paying for the three things I loved most: candle-lit dinners, clothing, and books (not necessarily in that order).

I remember panicking when I exceeded my credit limit the first time. What in the world was the bank going to do to me?

When the next bill arrived, I found out: it raised my credit limit. Incredibly, I was rewarded for breaking the rules! What power! What freedom!

What disaster.

Eighteen months later, two more important things happened to me: My marriage broke up, and I lost my job. But I still had my credit card, and by now the credit limit was all the way up to $1,500.

"When it is used properly, debt can actually create wealth."

I tried to go it alone for six months. I rented an apartment, got a job selling shoes, and generally tried to lead a normal life. But there was one problem: I was living well beyond my means. My paycheck covered my rent, the utilities bills, and my car payment. The credit card had to pay for everything else.

After six months, the bank had had enough. This time when I exceeded my limit, I received a notice demanding immediate payment of the amount over the limit, and they raised my required monthly minimum payment.

I did what any self-respecting 23-year-old would do under the circumstances: I moved back in with my parents, borrowed the money from them to pay off my credit card, and I went back to school.

The Purpose of Debt

Debt provides convenience, freedom, and flexibility in our lives. It allows us to buy goods and services by committing a portion of our future earnings to pay for them.

When it is used properly, debt can actually create wealth. Mortgages, for example, allow us to live in a house before it is fully paid for, and auto loans allow us to drive a car before the final payment is made.

There are really two kinds of debt: *mortgage debt*, and *installment debt.*

Do you know what the word *mortgage* means? The *American Heritage Dictionary* says it means "To pledge or stake against future success or failure; place an advance liability on." But if you read the fine print to find out where the word came from, it shows that *mortgage* is derived from a couple of Old Latin words: *mort*, meaning "dead," and *gage*, meaning "pledge." So the literal definition of *mortgage* is "dead pledge." (The early Latins must have seen the American real estate bust of the 1980s coming!)

Mortgage debt involves a loan that is secured by the property being purchased. In other words, if you stop making payments on your home, the mortgage lender can ultimately take possession of the home.

Installment debt involves *unsecured* loans. If you stop making payments on your credit card, the only alternative the card issuer has is to seek a legal judgment against you, forcing you to pay your balance. (The United States government, by the way, puts auto loans in the installment debt category even though lenders can repossess automobiles when borrowers are woefully behind in their payments.)

Mortgage lenders are normally very particular about who they lend money to. Borrowers must meet a number of rigorous financial standards in order to qualify for a loan. Installment debt, on the other hand, is relatively easy to incur. And that is where most people get themselves into financial difficulty (especially fiscally irresponsible 23-year-olds with $1,500 credit limits on credit cards who suddenly think they are J.D. Rockefeller).

So let's spend some time on installment debt and how to successfully manage it.

The History of Installment Debt in America

Legend has it that installment debt first came to America in 1856 when Isaac Singer allowed customers to take his $125 sewing machines home without fully paying for them. Instead, they set up a schedule of monthly payments.

It was the best thing that ever happened to American commerce. Increasing consumers' purchasing power by allowing them to "buy now and pay later" increased productivity a great deal. Manufacturers produced more, merchants sold more, consumers bought more...and the check was in the mail.

But allowing consumers to buy goods and services on time was also the worst thing to ever happen to American commerce. First, it increased the volatility of the business cycle by creating stronger expansions and deeper recessions. Consumers account for roughly two-thirds of American business activity. When they are buying, business is good. When they are buying with credit, business is very good. But when they stop buying, business is bad.

The second thing installment debt did was distort the American consumer's concept of affordability.

Before Isaac Singer, defining affordability was easy: you could afford something if you had the cash to pay for it. After Isaac Singer, affordability meant being able to make your monthly payments.

The First Credit Card

But even that concept changed in 1951. The Franklin National Bank of Long Island, New York, began issuing plastic cards that allowed cardholders to make purchases without using cash or checks. The credit card was born.

Initially, Franklin National required cardholders to pay their balances in full within 90 days, and it did not charge any interest or annual fees. But by 1958, after another 150 banks in the area had also issued credit cards, the competition for business forced banks to allow customers to pay off their balances over longer periods of time. Revolving debt had arrived.

Now it didn't matter if you could pay off your balance or not. The credit card company would carry the balance for you, for a price.

"Now it didn't matter if you could pay off your balance or not. The credit card company would carry the balance for you, for a price."

The Rise of Installment Debt

During the 1980s, Americans took on an unprecedented amount of installment debt. In 1982, for example, it accounted for roughly 12 percent of our total income. By 1988, it was soaking up close to 17 percent.

That contributed to the longest continuous peace-time expansion our economy has ever known.

But when we finally dropped from all the shopping, we stopped spending and started the painful process of paying off our debt. As a result, the economy went into a longer, deeper recession than normal that lasted through the late '80s and early '90s.

By the end of 1992, American consumers were carrying a balance of $743 billion in installment debt, or roughly 14.5 percent of their take-home pay.

Debt is power. If it is used wisely, it can be a useful budgeting tool. If it is not used wisely, it can be a financially destructive weapon.

Your Debt Management Plan

The problems I had with my first credit card are obvious: I didn't have a clear notion of what I could and could not afford, and I used the card to finance frivolous expenditures. What I sorely needed was a debt management plan.

A successful debt management plan has three parts:

1) You must first determine *how much* debt you can comfortably assume.

2) You must devise ground rules about *what* you will, and will not, use debt for.

3) You must have an *emergency* debt repayment plan in case something unforeseen happens to you.

"If, for example, your monthly net income is $2,000, you shouldn't devote more than $400 a month to things like auto and bank loans and credit card payments."

Part 1: How Much Debt Can You Afford?

The first step in putting a successful debt management plan together is to determine what your own personal debt ratio should be. That simply means figuring out what percentage of your monthly budget you can, and will, devote to installment debt payments.

Conventional wisdom says your debt ratio should be no higher than 20 percent. That means if, for example, your monthly net income is $2,000, you shouldn't devote more than $400 a month to things like auto and bank loans and credit card payments.

To me, determining how much debt you can assume is a matter of setting priorities.

First priority. You must first pay for necessities like housing, food, and utilities. In other words, make sure you have enough *Budget Dollars* to meet your monthly expenses. (See page 20 for a complete description of *Budget Dollars*.)

Second priority. Be sure to make your monthly contributions to your retirement account, your child's college fund, and your emergency reserve account. Those are your *Prosperity Dollars*. (*Prosperity Dollars* are discussed more thoroughly on page 20.)

Third priority. Make allowances for your miscellaneous check writing and cash expenditures.

Fourth priority. How much do you have left over?

Fifteen percent of your monthly take-home pay? Twenty percent? More? Less? Whatever it is, that is how much you should be able to devote to auto loans, credit cards, lines of credit, and other installment debt payments.

Putting installment debt payments at the bottom of your budget's priority list encourages you to save more, and as long as you stick to the plan it prohibits you from overextending yourself.

How to Determine Your Personal Debt Ratio
List your monthly net income. $ _____
List your monthly debt obligations. $ _____   (Do *not* include your mortgage.)
Divide your total monthly debt _____%   obligations into your monthly   net income.
If the result is around 15 percent, then you are close to the current national average. But a more prudent debt ratio — one that allows you to save more — might be closer to 10 percent.

Part 2: What Do You Use Debt For?

I cringe when I think of the number of fine meals I put on my credit card when I was a young man. Months after the memory of the dining experience had faded, I was still paying the bill. It was like taking out a 30-year mortgage on a house I was only going to use for a week.

A classic misuse of debt. (Thank heaven my second wife is an accountant!)

To manage your installment debt properly, divide it into two parts: shorter-term debt and longer-term debt.

Shorter-term debt. This is debt you should take no longer than one to three months to pay off. You incur shorter-term debt for one of two reasons:

1) Convenience. You can use it to pay for meals, clothing, gasoline, or other daily necessities, but only if you pay the tab at the end of the month. If you don't, you end up paying the credit card's finance charge.

2) Emergencies. You can dig your card out if you forget your checkbook, if you're short on cash, or if you're faced with an automotive or medical or other kind of emergency.

There are two kinds of plastic cards available to use for shorter-term debt: *credit cards*, of course, which allow you to pay your debts off in monthly installments, and *charge cards*, like the American Express Card, which require you to pay your monthly balance in full.

(Notice that I did not include debit, or cash/check, cards. These are the wave of the future. When you purchase something with a debit card, you are not taking on any debt because the bank that issued the card automatically deducts the amount of your purchase from your account the way a written check does. A number of gas stations, grocery stores, and fast-food outlets are starting to accept debit cards.)

Longer-term debt: This is debt you take up to 10 years to repay.

You use longer-term debt for:

1) *Big ticket items* like automobiles, or household appliances.

2) *Construction* of either an addition or an improvement to your home.

3) *Tuition costs* and expenses for your child's college education.

For longer-term debt, you can use lines of credit or bank loans. But remember: Don't let your monthly debt payments exceed the debt ratio limits you have set for yourself.

Part 3: How Will You Pay Your Debts in an Emergency?

Emergencies happen. Sometimes they temporarily halt your income, force you to divert your monthly expenditures, or drain your reserve accounts.

Your debt management plan should include an emergency debt repayment plan. Here are some of your alternatives:

1) If you have enough money in your reserve account, consider using it to pay your installment debts. But don't allow the account to become dangerously low.

Remember, your reserve account is there to pay for big ticket items, or to cover your monthly expenses for at least three to six months. (See page 27 for a more thorough discussion of creating a *reserve account*.)

2) Contact your creditors immediately and explain your situation. You won't be the first who has had to do it, and you won't be the last. Depending on the creditor and your history, you can either ask for a temporary moratorium on payments, or a period when you pay only the interest on what you owe, or some other arrangement.

3) Consider a bill consolidation loan. Depending on your creditworthiness, you may be able to secure a loan designed to pay off your other installment debts and leave you with a single, affordable monthly payment. Ask someone at your local bank branch.

4) You could borrow against your life insurance policy or your retirement plan at work. Most life insurance policies that include an investment feature (see page 159 for more details) allow you to borrow up to 95 percent of the cash portion of your policy. And some retirement plans, like 401(k)s, allow you to borrow a portion of the funds in your account.

5) If conditions are severe enough, you might consider filing for bankruptcy. But you should consider this option only after all others have failed. Consult an attorney who specializes in bankruptcies.

Note: At the end of this chapter, I have included the addresses and phone numbers of a couple of debt counseling organizations.

Shopping for Credit Cards

When you are shopping for a credit card, some features to consider are interest rate, annual fee, grace period, and rebates.

Interest Rate

In the credit card application's fine print, or disclosure section, the rate charged is usually listed as the APR, or Annual Percentage Rate. For years, most credit card issuers charged close to 20 percent. But after interest rates started to drop in the early '90s, and after aggressive new issuers hit the market, even leading credit card issuers like Citibank started to lower the rate they charged to finance existing credit balances.

Don't be fooled by interest rates listed in credit card advertisements. They are often an "introductory" rate that is good for the first six months you use the card. After that, the card's actual interest rate kicks in.

Some credit card rates are fixed, meaning they don't fluctuate with market conditions. Some cards now charge variable rates. They are usually tied to the prime rate, which is the interest rate a bank charges its most creditworthy customers. Most often, a variable rate will float 9–11 percent above the prime rate.

If you are the kind of person who does not pay your balance off each month, it would pay to shop around for the lowest interest rate you can find. (See the Who to Call section at the end of this chapter for the addresses and phone numbers of a couple of credit card tracking services.)

"Don't be fooled by interest rates listed in credit card advertisements. They are often an 'introductory' rate that is good for the first six months you use the card."

Annual Fee

In order to compensate for the lower rates they charge, some credit card issuers impose a fixed annual fee on customers. Some waive the fee if you simply use the card. But with all the competition out there, there really is no reason why you should have to pay an annual fee. Ask your current card issuer to waive it; otherwise, it is simple to find a credit card that doesn't charge one.

Grace Period

This is an important feature to know about. Most card issuers offer a grace period of around 25 days after a purchase is made before they impose a finance charge. Very simply, that means if you pay your bill in full when it arrives, you will not have to pay a finance charge.

There are some cards, though, where the finance charge clock begins to tick at the time of purchase. Look for this information in the fine print on the back of a credit card bill or application.

If you're the type of consumer who pays your credit card bill in full each month, you definitely should sign up for a credit card that offers a grace period.

Rebates

Some card issuers offer what they call "rebates" on most of your purchases. Some cards credit your account by a certain amount (usually 1 percent of the amount of your purchase). Other cards offer rebates that you can use for future purchases. After you have accumulated a certain dollar amount in your rebate account, you can use it toward the purchase of some goods and services.

Ford and General Motors, for example, both issue credit cards with rebates good toward the purchase of cars and trucks. And some commercial airlines offer frequent-flyer-type rebates that can be used for free round-trip tickets.

These are good deals if you use your card frequently and pay off your balance. If you don't pay the balance off, you could end up "spending" your rebates on finance charges.

Use Two Credit Cards

Consider using two credit cards.

Use one for shorter-term debt, like meals and clothing, that you plan to pay off each month. Make sure this card offers a grace period before it imposes a finance charge on your card's balance.

Use the other card for longer-term debt, for purchasing big ticket items like appliances and airline tickets. Find a credit card with the lowest interest rate around for this purpose since you will most likely be maintaining a balance.

Using two cards will help you to maintain the discipline of immediately paying off the smaller amounts you charge.

How Much Is Too Much Credit Card Debt?

I use two different barometers to determine how large a balance I should maintain on the credit card I use for longer-term debt:

1) *I never let my credit card balance exceed the amount I keep in my reserve account.* That way, I can always pay the credit card off instantly in case of an emergency.

2) *I try to keep my credit card balance at a level that I could pay off in at least 12 months,* finance charges and all, with the predetermined monthly credit card payment in my budget. (If, for example, I allot a $100 payment each month for my longer-term credit card, then I won't allow the balance on the card to exceed $1,200.) This prevents me from letting my credit card purchases get too out of hand.

Secured Credit Cards

If you haven't established a credit record yet, or if your credit record is a troubled one, you may still be able to receive a secured credit card from a bank.

With this kind of card, the bank will require you to deposit a certain amount of money (usually $400) that acts as your credit limit.

If, for example, you deposit $2,000 with the bank, your secured credit card will have a limit of $2,000.

Secured cards are not usually a very good deal. They charge rather high interest rates, and they usually involve annual fees. But they do allow you to establish, or reestablish, a credit record.

Once you have established enough of a track record to qualify for a traditional credit card, you would be well advised to get rid of the secured card.

Using Your Home Equity to Secure Credit

When Congress eliminated the tax deductibility of credit card interest with the Tax Reform Act of 1986, banks and other lenders developed ways for consumers to secure tax deductible loans based on the amount of equity they had built up in their homes.

Today, there are two ways to borrow against the equity in your home, home equity lines of credit and home equity credit cards.

Home Equity Lines of Credit

Home equity lines of credit are usually opened through a bank. They look and feel just like a regular checking account, but you should never forget that your home is on the line. If you don't pay back what you've borrowed, you could lose your home.

Securing a home equity line of credit is just like taking out a mortgage. Your credit record must be in order, your debt ratio must not be too high, and you have to pay the usual points and fees associated with securing a mortgage.

The size of your line of credit will be determined by the amount of equity you have built up in your home. Here is how the math works: The lender takes a percentage (usually 75 percent) of the appraised value of your home and subtracts whatever you still owe on your mortgage.

For example:

Appraised value of your home	*$100,000*
	x 75%
Percentage of appraised value	*$75,000*
Less existing mortgage debt	*$60,000*
Potential credit line	*$15,000*

The interest charged on a home equity line of credit is almost always a variable rate tied to some index related to what Treasury securities yield.

Home Equity Credit Cards

You knew it would eventually come to this. Early in 1993, a few aggressive regional banks started issuing credit cards tied to home equity.

The good news is that consumers who use the cards can deduct interest expenses from their taxes. And the interest charged is much lower than what banks charge for traditional credit cards because home equity credit card rates are essentially the same as mortgage rates.

The bad news is the up-front fees can be quite high (getting a home equity credit card is just like taking out another mortgage), and a delinquent account could eventually result in the credit card issuer seizing possession of your home.

Your Credit Record

My wife and I once received a letter from TRW Information Services, one of the country's leading credit bureaus, telling us that a loan we had applied for at a local jewelry store had been denied.

The problem was we hadn't applied for a loan at any jewelry store. It turned out that an overly ambitious employee who was trying to win a sales contest had taken it upon himself to submit a number of phantom loan applications using information the store had on file about customers who had purchased items at the store in the past. (Our "application," by the way, was turned down by TRW because the employee had submitted incorrect information. He couldn't even get that part right!)

Our first order of business was to demand that the jewelry store explain what had happened to TRW Information Services, so that the loan application denial could be stricken from our credit record.

A clean credit record is a valuable asset. When you apply for a loan, an insurance policy, or even a job, your prospective creditor or employer heads for your credit record to obtain objective information about you.

Your credit record is kept by three major credit reporting agencies: TRW Consumer Credit Services, Equifax, and Trans Union. Each of them keeps a record of your mortgage loans, auto loans, credit card accounts, lines of credit, and rental agreements.

Note: I have listed the addresses and phone numbers of each of these services in the Who to Call section at the end of this chapter.

Each time you make a payment, your creditor reports it to these agencies. They also report any payments you may miss. If a collection agency ever gets involved with any of your accounts because you have fallen behind in your payments, it will show up on your credit record. So will a bankruptcy.

It is vitally important that you periodically review a copy of your credit record to make sure the information in it is accurate. Each of the credit reporting agencies will send you a copy when you send them a written request.

"It is vitally important that you periodically review a copy of your credit record to make sure the information in it is accurate."

What's in a Credit Record?

Your credit record includes your name, Social Security number, and your current and former addresses for the previous five years. It will also list your current and former employers for the previous five years.

Your record also lists all loans and credit card accounts you have outstanding, when the loans and accounts were opened, the size of the loans and the limits on the credit cards, your current outstanding balances on each, whether you are up-to-date with your payments, and when your last payment was recorded.

Finally, your record also lists recent inquiries made by potential creditors.

Who Has Access to Your Credit Record?

It used to bother me when it seemed that any vendor could gain access to my credit record for any reason. But I have since discovered that it is not quite that easy.

Yes, potential creditors can gain access to your credit record. But first they are screened by the credit bureaus to make sure they are making legitimate inquiries. And all potential creditors are required to sign an agreement with the bureaus, requiring them to keep your credit records confidential.

Here is a list of who has access to your credit record:

- *Current creditors.* As I said before, they report all your payments to the agencies. And when credit card issuers want to raise your credit limit, first they take a peek at your credit record to make sure you warrant it.

- *Potential employers.* They review your record mainly to verify your employment history for the past five years and to make sure you actually live where you say you do.

- *Potential landlords.* They are making sure you pay your bills on time and that you don't have too many outstanding debts competing with the rent money.

- *Insurance companies.* When you apply for an insurance policy, insurers verify the name of your current address and employer, and they check for a consistent bill payment record.

- *Mailing lists.* Yes, this is sometimes where they get your name. But you should be aware that if you do not want the credit bureaus to give your name to any mailing lists, you can make such a request in writing.

What If You Disagree with Something in Your Credit Record?

If you feel something in your credit record is incorrect, you must send documents to the reporting agency to prove your point. If it turns out that you are correct, the reporting agency will delete the incorrect information and send you a new corrected version of your credit report.

If it turns out that the information in question is correct, you are entitled to send the credit reporting agency your written version of the story — it must be 100 words or less — and it will be attached to your credit report for all creditors and potential creditors to see.

Credit Repair Agencies

Watch out for companies that claim they can "repair" your credit report if you have accumulated too many negatives. The fact is *no one* can repair an accurate, negative credit report. And any company that makes that claim should be reported to the Better Business Bureau.

How Long Do Negative Entries Remain in a Credit Report?

The Fair Credit Reporting Act requires credit bureaus to list negative entries in your report for seven years. Bankruptcy filings must remain for ten years (except for completed Chapter 13 filings, which remain for seven years).

Summary

A successful debt management plan gives you enough flexibility to meet unexpected emergencies or to take advantage of unexpected opportunities.

Debt reduces that flexibility. And too much debt kills it altogether.

Who to Call

Credit Card Tracking Services

These two companies keep track of who is offering credit cards, and how much they are charging. Both services offer newsletters that highlight trends in the credit card industry, and they list credit cards with the lowest interest rates, credit cards that do and do not offer grace periods, credit cards that do and do not charge annual fees, and other features.

Both of these credit card tracking services provide solid information.

Ram Research. Ram Research publishes a monthly newsletter called *CardTrak.* For subscription information:

> *Ram Research*
> P.O. Box 1700 (College Estates)
> Frederick, MD 21702
> (301) 695–4660
> (800) 344–7714 (for a taped message about how to subscribe)

Bankcard Holders of America. This organization provides subscribers with lists of banks that offer credit cards with various features. It also publishes a number of brochures with titles like: "Consumer Credit Rights," "How To Re-establish Good Credit," "Credit Secrets Manual," and "Women's Credit Rights," among others.

For information:

> *Bankcard Holders of America*
> 560 Herndon Parkway Suite 120
> Herndon, VA 22070
> (800) 553–8025
> (703) 481–1110

Credit Card Issuers

Mastercard International. Mastercard has a couple of *free* brochures available: "Credit Card Basics," and "Credit Card Fraud." (800) 999–5136

Visa International. Visa's *free* credit card brochure is called: "Credit Cards: An Owner's Manual." (800) 847–2511

Credit Bureaus

These are the three largest credit bureaus in the country. In order to receive a copy of your current record, you *must* submit your request in writing. Some services charge a fee, some do not.

> *TRW Information Services*
> P.O. Box 2101
> Allen, TX 75002–2101
> (800) 262–7432

> *Equifax Credit Information Services*
> P.O. Box 740241
> Atlanta, GA 30374–0241
> (404) 885–8231
> (800) 685–1111

> *Trans Union's National Consumer Relations Disclosure Center*
> 212 S. Market
> Wichita, KS 67202
> (312) 258–1717

Debt Counseling Services

There are a number of services around the country that help people get their spending habits under control and create a workable debt repayment plan. Here are a couple of examples:

The National Foundation for Consumer Credit. This organization has nonprofit credit counseling services all over the country.

> 8611 Second Ave. Suite 100
> Silver Spring, MD 20910
> (301) 589–5600
> (800) 388–2227

Debtors Anonymous. This organization offers a program much like Alcoholics Anonymous. It has local support groups all over the country.

> *General Service Board*
> P.O. Box 400
> Grand Central Station
> New York, NY 10163-0400
> (212) 969–8111

STEP 6

Develop a Do-It-Yourself Retirement Plan
Start saving NOW!

Saving money for a down payment on a home is exciting. And saving money for a child's college education is a parent's solemn duty.

Saving for retirement? That won't happen for a long time, so it can wait.

That was the message from people who responded to a couple of surveys conducted by Fidelity Investments in 1992 and 1993.

In the first survey, 1,400 Americans were asked if they were willing to reduce their personal spending in order to save more for retirement. A whopping 74 percent said yes.

One year later in the second survey, another 1,400 were asked the same question. This time only 54 percent said they were willing to cut spending in order to save for retirement.

Among the other findings in Fidelity's surveys:

- *72 percent* of those polled in the first survey said they would reduce dining-out costs in order to save for retirement, but only 31 percent said they would in the second survey.

- *67 percent* of those polled in the first survey said they would cut entertainment and leisure activities, but only one-third said the same thing in the second.

Why the change of heart? Fidelity's economists concluded that the condition of the economy dictated most people's willingness to save for retirement. When the economy is in recession, as it was in 1992, it scares people into thinking about preparing for future rainy days. But when the economy is expanding, as it was starting to do in 1993, people tend to forget about the hard times and start spending again.

Roger Servison, the managing director at Fidelity, summed up the survey's findings by stating the obvious: "Unless personal savings increase, Americans may have to accept lower standards of living in retirement."

Indeed, saving for retirement has never been more important. And the earlier you start, the more comfortable your retirement years will be.

"Indeed, saving for retirement has never been more important. And the earlier you start, the more comfortable your retirement years will be."

When Should I Start Saving for Retirement?

How about today?

And if you start early enough, you don't have to save a lot of money each month.

Could you afford to pay yourself $1 a day? That's $30–$31 a month, or $365 a year. And if you invest your money in an equity mutual fund that earns, say, an average annual compounded yield of 7 percent, in 30 years your nest egg will be $34,474.25.

Could you do better than $1 a day? Table 6-1 shows how much you could accumulate in 30 years, with that 7 percent average annual compounded yield, if you paid yourself up to $10 a day.

Table 6-1

Pay Yourself	Nest Egg in 30 Years
$1 a Day	$34,474.25
$2 a Day	$68,948.50
$3 a Day	$103,422.75
$4 a Day	$137,897.00
$5 a Day	$172,371.25
$6 a Day	$206,845.50
$7 a Day	$241,319.15
$8 a Day	$275,794.00
$9 a Day	$310,268.25
$10 a Day	$344,742.50

source: *SteinRoe & Farnham*

You must understand that the 7 percent compounded return is not guaranteed, but it is not unreasonable either. The point of the exercise is to give you an idea of what is possible to accumulate when you start with a very small amount of money.

Tax-Deferred Savings Versus Taxable Savings

Your nest egg will be even larger if your money grows tax free.

The government allows your retirement savings to grow on a tax-deferred basis if you invest in what are called *qualified retirement plans* (which I will get to later in the chapter). You don't pay taxes on the money your account earns until you withdraw it during retirement, when your tax bracket will presumably be lower than it is while you're working.

Your money grows a lot faster when it is earning tax-deferred income.

TAXABLE VERSUS TAX-DEFERRED INVESTMENTS

$2,000/yr. after 25 years earning 7%

Taxable: $97,751

Tax-Deferred: $135,353

Difference: $37,602

Let's assume you save $2,000 a year (that's roughly $5.50 a day). If you invested the money in an equity mutual fund that returned 7 percent a year, and you had to pay taxes on the earned income, after 25 years your nest egg would be worth $97,751.

If, on the other hand, you invested the $2,000 each year in a qualified individual retirement account (IRA), which does not require you to pay taxes on the earned income until you withdraw the money in retirement, after 25 years (with the 7 percent annual return) your nest egg would be worth $135,353. That's a difference of $37,602.

Surveys show that most people save for retirement the way they used to study for final exams: They wait until the last minute. The earlier you start saving for retirement, the less of a burden it will be on your monthly budget over time.

How Much Money Will You Need to Retire on?

A study released in early 1994 by the Municipal Bond Investor Assurance Corporation (MBIA) — the folks who insure municipal bonds — asked members of the Baby Boom generation how much of a nest egg they thought they would need to retire on. Of those who responded, 34 percent said they would need up to $500,000, 29 percent didn't know how much they would need, and 19 percent figured they could get by on less than $100,000.

"The problem is, with today's low interest rates, a $500,000 nest egg would only produce an income of $1,500 a month or $18,000 a year (assuming a safe 4 percent yield)."

BABY BOOMER SURVEY

How Much of a Nest Egg Will You Need to Retire on?

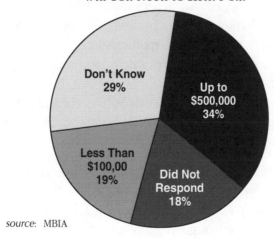

source: MBIA

The problem is, with today's low interest rates, a $500,000 nest egg would only produce an income of $1,500 a month or $18,000 a year *(assuming a safe 4 percent yield)*. In order to achieve the same level of income with a $100,000 nest egg, you would need your investments to yield 18 percent!

Eighteen thousand dollars may sound like a retirement income you could live with right now (especially if you have Social Security to supplement it). But in 15–30 years, $18,000 will most likely be below the government's official poverty level, and Social Security may be out of business.

"In 15–30 years, $18,000 will most likely be below the government's official poverty level, and Social Security may be out of business."

Determining how much money you will need to save in order to retire comfortably is both an art and a science.

It's an art because there really is no way of knowing *exactly* how much you will need to retire on, especially if you aren't planning to retire for 15–30 years or more. No one knows what the cost of living will be that far in the future. We can only guess.

There is a science to determining what size nest egg you will require at retirement, though. Financial planners use complicated mathematical models that try to anticipate future economic conditions between now and when you retire. Things like the rate of inflation, the level of interest rates, the kind of return you should expect from investments in the stock market, and your income level.

To ballpark it, though, financial planners generally say that if you're between the ages of 35 and 50 (presumably your peak earning years), you should expect to live on roughly 70 percent of your current income.

The theory is that when you retire, your expenses are reduced because you have probably paid off your mortgage by then, and you don't have work-related expenses to cover like your professional wardrobe, your travel expenses to and from work, and all the meals you paid for in the company cafeteria.

So how much money will you need to provide that level of income?

Tables 6-2 and 6-3 should help you determine that. This is a simple five-step system devised by the folks at the Delaware Group of Mutual Funds in Philadelphia.

Here is how it works:

Step 1. Find your current annual salary in the first column of Table 6-2.

Step 2. Decide what percentage of your current income you could live on in retirement and find the column that corresponds with that percentage.

Step 3. Move down that column and find the monthly income figure on the same line with your annual salary.

Step 4. Estimate what you think your nest egg will yield when you retire. (If you're still 15–30 years from retirement, this is a real guessing game. To be safe, use a conservative estimate of 4 or 6 percent. That will force you to build a larger nest egg.)

Step 5. In Table 6-3 find the "Principal Factor" under the interest rate you choose and multiply it by your monthly income figure from Table 6-2.

Example: Let's assume current annual income is $30,000, and you feel you will be able to retire comfortably if your nest egg is able to produce 70 percent of your current income. Table 6-2 shows that your nest egg will need to produce $1,750 a month in order to achieve 70 percent of your current income.

Table 6-2

Salary before Retirement	Monthly Income from Salary	% of Pre-Retirement Income Desired from Your Savings									
		50%	55%	60%	65%	70%	75%	80%	85%	90%	95%
$25,000	$2,083	$1,042	$1,146	$1,250	$1,354	$1,458	$1,563	$1,667	$1,771	$1,875	$1,979
$30,000	$2,500	$1,250	$1,375	$1,500	$1,625	$1,750	$1,875	$2,000	$2,125	$2,250	$2,375
$35,000	$2,917	$1,458	$1,604	$1,750	$1,896	$2,042	$2,188	$2,333	$2,479	$2,625	$2,771
$40,000	$3,333	$1,667	$1,833	$2,000	$2,167	$2,333	$2,500	$2,667	$2,833	$3,000	$3,167
$45,000	$3,750	$1,875	$2,063	$2,250	$2,438	$2,625	$2,813	$3,000	$3,188	$3,375	$3,563
$50,000	$4,167	$2,083	$2,292	$2,500	$2,708	$2,917	$3,125	$3,333	$3,542	$3,750	$3,958
$55,000	$4,583	$2,292	$2,521	$2,750	$2,979	$3,208	$3,438	$3,667	$3,896	$4,125	$4,354
$60,000	$5,000	$2,500	$2,750	$3,000	$3,250	$3,500	$3,750	$4,000	$4,250	$4,500	$4,750
$65,000	$5,417	$2,708	$2,979	$3,250	$3,521	$3,792	$4,063	$4,333	$4,604	$4,875	$5,146
$70,000	$5,833	$2,917	$3,208	$3,500	$3,792	$4,083	$4,375	$4,667	$4,958	$5,250	$5,542
$75,000	$6,250	$3,125	$3,438	$3,750	$4,063	$4,375	$4,688	$5,000	$5,313	$5,625	$5,938
$80,000	$6,667	$3,333	$3,667	$4,000	$4,333	$4,667	$5,000	$5,333	$5,667	$6,000	$6,333
$85,000	$7,083	$3,542	$3,896	$4,250	$4,604	$4,958	$5,313	$5,667	$6,021	$6,375	$6,729
$90,000	$7,500	$3,750	$4,125	$4,500	$4,875	$5,250	$5,625	$6,000	$6,375	$6,750	$7,125
$95,000	$7,917	$3,958	$4,354	$4,750	$5,146	$5,542	$5,938	$6,333	$6,729	$7,125	$7,521
$100,000	$8,333	$4,167	$4,583	$5,000	$5,417	$5,833	$6,250	$6,667	$7,083	$7,500	$7,917
$105,000	$8,760	$4,375	$4,813	$5,250	$5,688	$6,125	$6,563	$7,000	$7,438	$7,875	$8,313
$110,000	$9,167	$4,583	$5,042	$5,500	$5,958	$6,417	$6,875	$7,333	$7,792	$8,250	$8,708
$115,000	$9,583	$4,792	$5,271	$5,750	$6,229	$6,708	$7,188	$7,667	$8,146	$8,625	$9,104
$120,000	$10,000	$5,000	$5,500	$6,000	$6,500	$7,000	$7,500	$8,000	$8,500	$9,000	$9,500
$125,000	$10,417	$5,208	$5,729	$6,250	$6,771	$7,292	$7,813	$8,333	$8,854	$9,375	$9,896

source: The Delaware Group of Mutual Funds

Table 6-3

Market Interest Rate	Principal Factor
2.00%	600.00
4.00%	300.00
6.00%	200.00
8.00%	150.00
10.00%	120.00
12.00%	100.00
14.00%	85.7143
16.00%	75.00
18.00%	66.6667
20.00%	60.00

source: *The Delaware Group of Mutual Funds*

Now let's assume that you estimate the financial markets will allow your nest egg to produce a 6 percent return on investment when you retire. In Table 6-3, the principal factor corresponding to 6 percent is 200.

$$\begin{array}{r} \$1,750 \\ \times \quad 200 \\ \hline \$350,000 \end{array}$$

You would need to build a nest egg of at least $350,000 to provide you with a monthly income of $1,750. And that, by the way, would be interest-only income. You would not have to withdraw any of the principal from your nest egg.

You must understand that we are only talking about rough estimates here. And don't forget that economic and market conditions can change. If interest rates drop, as they did in the early 1990s, your nest egg won't earn as much, and you could find yourself withdrawing a portion of your principal to meet expenses.

And because people are generally living longer than they used to, your nest egg may have to last you as long as 20–25 years.

That is why it is so important to start saving for retirement immediately. Save as much as you can afford, and invest whatever the government allows in tax-deferred retirement plans.

Good-Bye Pensions: Hello Do-It-Yourself Retirement Plans

Once upon a time in America, employers told their employees, "If you are a good and faithful worker, and if you serve us for a long time, we will continue to pay you when you retire."

That is known as a *pension*. (The word comes from the Old French, meaning "payment.") The technical term for this type of pension is a *defined benefit plan*.

Pensions were first introduced in America in 1875 by the American Express Company. But they didn't really catch on in this country until the 20th century. (According to the Pension Benefit Guaranty Corporation, which insures pension plans, there were 65,000 plans with pension liabilities of $235 billion by the end of 1992, when the most recent data were available.)

In 1935 the federal government introduced its own pension-like program for citizens, known as Social Security.

When you combined a company pension with Social Security, it was a pretty good deal. And if you had saved some money on your own, chances are you were in terrific shape financially when you retired.

But something happened on the way to Sun City. Economic conditions and demographics changed:

- *People started living longer,* and companies found they were paying more retirees than workers. Bethlehem Steel is a good example. In 1993, the company was paying pension benefits to 77,000 retirees. At the same time, it only employed 22,000 workers. Bethlehem Steel wasn't in the steel business anymore. It was in the pension business.

- *Economic conditions forced some companies to borrow money* from their employees' pension funds in order to keep going. And when things didn't improve, the money wasn't returned to the funds. The result: Corporate pensions in the United States were underfunded by $53 billion by the end of 1992. (I should point out that roughly three-quarters of the underfunding was concentrated in just 50 companies, primarily in the steel, auto, tire, and airline industries.)

The bottom line was this: It didn't make sense for companies to offer pensions to workers anymore.

So in the 1970s, employers started telling employees that if they would contribute a portion of their paycheck to a retirement account, the employer would match all or a portion of that contribution.

These plans are known as *defined contribution plans.*

Defined contribution plans are on the rise, and defined benefit plans are slowly disappearing: In 1975, old-fashioned pension plans covered 27.2

million workers, while the new plans covered 11.2 million participants. By 1990, 38.5 million Americans were putting money in the new plans, while only 28.8 million were covered by the old plans. And by 1996, the amount of money in the new plans is expected to exceed the amount in the old plans.

"By 1990, 38.5 million Americans were putting money in the new plans, while only 28.8 million were covered by the old plans."

So we are now responsible for paying for our own retirement, especially now that Social Security is expected to have financial problems in the next century (which I will get to later in this chapter).

The do-it-yourself retirement plan is here, and the sooner you start one, the more pleasant your golden years will be.

Do-It-Yourself Retirement Plans

The good news about saving for retirement is there are a number of plans to choose from, and they are convenient and inexpensive.

Individual Retirement Account (IRA)

IRA is the government's version of your employer's defined contribution plan. When it became evident that Social Security was going to start running out of money very early in the next century, the government introduced Individual Retirement Accounts in the early 1980s.

The idea was that everyone could contribute up to $2,000 each year to an IRA. We could deduct all or part of the contribution from our income taxes, and we wouldn't have to pay taxes on whatever the IRA earned until we began withdrawing the money when we retired.

Remember when IRAs were first introduced? Advertisements boasted that if a 25-year-old started contributing $2,000 a year to an IRA, by the time he or she reached age 65, his or her account would probably be worth a cool $1 million. (What the ads didn't say was that by the time a 25-year-old in 1980 hit retirement age in the year 2020, he or she would probably need $2 million to retire on.)

At any rate, in 1986 the government changed the laws governing IRAs. The tax reform act passed that year said that you could no longer take the full tax deduction for your annual IRA contribution if:

1) *You (or your spouse) were already covered* by an employer sponsored retirement plan.

OR

2) *Your annual adjusted gross income was more than $35,000* (if you're single) or $50,000 (if you're married filing a joint return).

That immediately took some of the top spin off the IRA boom of the early '80s. But the market is still huge. By the end of 1992, Americans had invested $725 billion in IRAs.

One of the quirks of the laws governing IRAs is that you have until April 15 to open one or to complete your $2,000 contribution, in order to take the tax deduction for the previous year (assuming you qualify for the tax deduction).

Keogh Plan

Keogh plans are for self-employed individuals who want to set up a retirement fund for themselves. They are named for United States Representative Eugene Keogh, who introduced them in the 1960s.

Keoghs are pretty flexible when it comes to contributions. You can choose to contribute a fixed percentage of your annual income (up to $30,000), or a variable portion of your earnings, or nothing at all. (But you must stick with one plan. You can't contribute a fixed percentage of income one year, for example, and then choose to contribute a variable amount the next year.)

The only restriction is you are allowed to contribute only self-employment income.

Unlike an IRA, you must open a Keogh Plan by December 31 in order to qualify for your tax deduction. (Although you still have until April 15 of the following year to make your full annual contribution and still qualify for the tax deduction.)

401(k) and 403(b) and 457

These are defined contribution plans offered by most employers. They allow employees to contribute a combination of taxable and pretax dollars (up to $8,994 in 1993) into an account that offers at least three types of investments (typically mutual funds that invest in stocks, bonds, and money market instruments). Some employers will match all or a portion of an employee's contribution.

- *401(k) plans* are for people employed by companies with 25 or more employees.

- *403(b) plans* are for people who work for not-for-profit organizations, such as charities or school systems.

- *457 plans* are for government employees.

(The plans' numerical designations, by the way, refer to the paragraph numbers in the Internal Revenue Code where these retirement plans are described.)

In 1992, the government passed a law that makes defined contribution plans true do-it-yourself retirement programs.

Essentially, the law — known in the industry as section 404(c) of the Employee Retirement Income Security Act (or ERISA) — says that employers must provide employees with at least three investment options in their defined contribution plans, and they must give employees enough information about those investments so that the employees can make their own investment decisions.

What that means is employers are not allowed to give investment advice to their employees, and neither are the people who manage the investments for the retirement accounts. *You are on your own.*

Simplified Employee Pension (SEP) Plans

These are defined contribution plans for people who work for companies with 25 or fewer employees.

If your employer has 25 or fewer employees, at least half of the employees must enroll in the SEP in order for it to become effective. Then — just as with a 401(k) — each employee is allowed to contribute a combination of taxable and pretax dollars (up to $8,994 in 1993) into an investment account where the earnings are tax deferred until the money is withdrawn.

If you are the sole employee of a company, a SEP acts more like an IRA or a Keogh, in that you can contribute up to 15 percent of your annual income (or a maximum of $30,000).

And, like an IRA and a Keogh, you are not allowed to borrow any money from your SEP. (You are, however, allowed to borrow from your 401(k).)

Note: You are subject to an additional 10 percent tax by the IRS if you withdraw money from any defined contribution plan before you reach age 59 1/2.

"People tend to be too conservative with the money they invest for retirement."

Investing Your Retirement Savings

Wally is a 26-year-old fitness trainer. He is generally a pretty aggressive fellow. He works hard to stay in top physical condition, and he urges his clients to do the same.

But when we profiled Wally on CNBC in early 1994, we found that when it came to saving for his retirement, he was pretty conservative.

"It's the money I'm going to need when I stop working," he told us. "So I don't want to risk losing any of it."

His heart was in the right place, but at age 26, Wally's greatest risk is not in *losing money*. It is *not earning enough in his retirement account to keep up with the rate of inflation.*

People tend to be too conservative with the money they invest for retirement. A study conducted by the people who manage pension money for Los Angeles County government employees found a startling difference between the portfolios built by professional pension fund managers and those built by the county employees themselves (see Figure 6-1).

Figure 6-1

HOW DO THEY INVEST RETIREMENT SAVINGS?

Pension Fund Managers

Other 12%

Fixed-Income (Bonds) 29%

Diversified Stocks 59%

Savings Plan Participants

Investment Contracts 49%

Other 36%

Fixed-Income (Bonds) 1%

Diversified Stock Funds 14%

source: *L.A. County Employees' Saving Plan Newsletter*

The study found that employees were much more conservative with their asset allocation than the professional pension fund managers were.

By being too conservative, the employees were actually hurting themselves. Consider what happens to a retiree who withdraws the same amount of money each year from savings when inflation averages about 5 percent a year. The amount the retiree receives in the 14th year of retirement will be worth only half what it was in the first year of retirement.

In order to keep up with the rising cost of living, you must take some risk with your retirement savings. (Refer to the Lifetime Investment Plan outlined in Chapter 3 for a suggested retirement portfolio.)

What About Social Security?

On August 14, 1935, President Franklin Roosevelt signed Social Security into law in order to provide most Americans with a guaranteed supplement to their retirement income at the height of the Great Depression.

The idea was simple: The government would tax working Americans and use the money to pay retired Americans.

The idea was also very successful. By 1945, 46 working Americans were paying *into* Social Security for every retired American being paid *by* Social Security. It was a very comfortable ratio that virtually guaranteed the system's future. But over the next 50 years a number of things occurred that put that future in doubt.

1) *Congress periodically broadened the definition* of who was eligible for Social Security benefits, including disabled Americans and minors. That reduced the worker/retiree ratio. By 1950, it was down to 16:1.

2) *The size of the Baby Boom generation* certainly helped improve the ratio because of the vast number of taxable Americans it brought to the work force. But the bad news is that the Boomers are followed by the much smaller Baby Bust generation, the 35 million Americans born between 1965 and 1975. So by the year 2025, when the majority of Boomers are retired, it is expected that there will be only *two workers* paying into Social Security for every one retiree receiving Social Security benefits!

3) Congressional accounting procedures haven't helped, either. Social Security has been running a surplus for a number of years. But here is what Congress has done with that surplus: Instead of investing the money and letting it grow with compounded interest in order to meet the heavier load expected when the Boomer generation retires, the government has instead used the surplus to buy Treasury bills. The interest those T-bills pay is then used to help pay the government's *current* bills.

So the Social Security surplus is slowly disappearing, and it is anticipated that the Social Security Administration will actually begin to run at a deficit by the year 2011, the very same year the Baby Boom generation begins to retire.

It's no wonder a survey conducted for Merrill Lynch in late 1992 found that 85 percent of Baby Boomers do not expect Social Security to be their most important source of retirement income. The Investment Company Institute has determined that by the year 2000, Social Security will contribute only 15 cents of every retirement dollar. And unless government accounting methods and/or tax laws change, Social Security will contribute far less than that when the Boomers retire.

But let's assume Social Security will be there for the Boomer generation in some form. (A booklet published in 1993 by the Social Security Administration projected that the SSA trust funds were good for at least another 45 years.) You should get to know how Social Security works, and what it will — and will *not* — be able to do for you now and in the future.

"It is anticipated that the Social Security Administration will actually begin to run at a deficit by the year 2011, the very same year the Baby Boom generation begins to retire."

How Social Security Works

During your working years, you pay taxes to the Social Security Administration. It is normally itemized on your check as a FICA contribution. FICA stands for Federal Insurance Contributions Act, which is the law that authorized Social Security payroll deductions. Your tax contributions are placed into three different trust funds (Figure 6-2).

Figure 6-2

THE THREE SOCIAL SECURITY TRUST FUNDS

One trust fund is used to finance two kinds of Social Security benefits:

1) Retirement. The traditional form of Social Security benefits.

2) Survivors. These are Social Security benefits paid to certain members of your family when you die. A pamphlet published by the SSA called "Understanding Social Security" lists family members who may be eligible for survivor benefits:

- A widow or widower who is 60 or older.

- A widow or widower who is 50 or older and disabled.

- A widow or widower at any age if she or he is caring for a child under 16 or a disabled child who is also receiving Social Security benefits.

- Children if they are unmarried and under 18.

- Children if they are unmarried and under 19 but in an elementary or secondary school as a full-time student.

- Children who are 18 or older and severely disabled, and the disability must have started before age 22.

- Your parents, if they were dependent on you for at least half of their support.

A second trust fund is used to finance *disability benefits*. The Social Security Administration says if you become disabled to the point where you are unable to work at a job that pays at least $500 a month, you may be eligible for disability benefits. And certain members of your family may also qualify under your account.

The third trust fund finances the benefits paid under the *Medicare* system, which is the government's basic health care insurance program for people who are 65 or older, and for many people who are disabled. (See pages 172–173 for a more thorough explanation of Medicare.)

How Social Security Benefits Are Calculated

It is important to note that the tax money you pay is *not* earmarked directly for your retirement. It is used to pay current retirees. Your Social Security retirement benefits will be paid by the people who are working when you retire.

I mention this because some people may hold the misconception that they will receive from the Social Security trust fund exactly what they paid into it. That is not true. (In fact, the first person ever to receive

Social Security benefits, back in the '30s, reportedly paid only $22 into the system. Social Security ended up paying her a total of $20,000 during her retirement until her death at age 99.)

Figure 6-3

"Some people may hold the misconception that they will receive from the Social Security trust fund exactly what they paid into it."

How Social Security Benefits Are Calculated

- **– Number of years worked**

- **– Amount of money earned**

- **– Your age when you retire**

To determine how much Social Security will pay you when you retire, the system considers three things (Figure 6-3):

1) The number of years you worked. The Social Security Administration measures your working life in terms of credits: You essentially earn 4 credits for every year worked, and you must earn 40 credits in order to qualify for Social Security retirement benefits.

2) The amount of money you earned during your working life. Social Security taxes salary and wages up to a certain amount. From 1937 to 1950, for example, workers were taxed on the first $3,000 they earned each year. In 1951 the limit was raised to $3,600, and it has gradually increased through the years.

In 1993, the salary limit was $57,600. So if you made less than $57,600 in 1993, you paid taxes to Social Security on every dollar you made. If you made more, you were only taxed on the first $57,600 you earned.

Medicare contributions have a higher salary limit. In 1993, it was $135,000.

3) Your age when you decide to start receiving retirement benefits. You have three kinds of retirement to choose from: full retirement, early retirement, and delayed retirement.

Full Retirement

The Social Security Administration allows you to begin receiving what it determines to be your full retirement benefits when you reach *full retirement age.* For years that age was 65. But in order to ease the expected future burden on the Social Security trust funds, the government has gradually increased the legal full retirement age for people born after 1938.

Table 6-4 outlines when you will be able to start receiving full retirement benefits from Social Security.

Table 6-4

WHAT IS YOUR FULL RETIREMENT AGE?

Year of Birth	Full Retirement Age
1937 or earlier	65
1938	65 + 2 months
1939	65 + 4 months
1940	65 + 6 months
1941	65 + 8 months
1942	65 +10 months
1943–1954	66
1955	66 + 2 months
1956	66 + 4 months
1957	66 + 6 months
1958	66 + 8 months
1959	66 +10 months
1960 and later	67

Early Retirement

If you choose to retire before your legal full retirement age, you can begin receiving Social Security retirement benefits as early as age 62.

But if you do, your monthly check will always be 20–25 percent less than your full retirement check would have been, depending on what your particular legal full retirement age is.

Even if you don't need the money yet at age 62, you might think about taking your reduced early retirement benefits, especially if it doesn't appreciably increase your tax burden, and investing it.

Here is why:

1) You could take control of your money as soon as possible and have it available for emergencies.

2) You could conceivably earn a better rate of return on the money than the Social Security trust fund could.

You should consult with a tax accountant, though, to decide if it makes sense for you.

Delayed Retirement

If you wait to take your Social Security retirement benefits until you reach age 70, your monthly check will always be 15–20 percent more than your full retirement check would have been, again depending on what your particular legal full retirement age is.

If you decide to work beyond your legal full retirement age, and if your income is high enough to comfortably support you, it might make sense to take the delayed retirement benefits.

How Much Will Social Security Pay You When You Retire?

You can find out today, no matter how far away you may be from your legal retirement age. The Social Security Administration will send you an estimate of what you will probably be paid when you retire.

The toll-free number to call is: 1–800–772–1213.

The menu-driven voice-mail system will ask you for your name, address, Social Security number, and the state you live in. The SSA then sends you an application for a free *Personal Earnings and Benefit Estimate Statement.*

Fill it out, send it in, and about four weeks later you will receive a personalized brochure that outlines how much you have paid into Social Security every year you have worked, how many credits you have earned so far, and an estimate of how much your retirement, disability, and survivors' benefits would be in today's dollars.

Social Security Booklets

The Social Security Administration offers a number of free booklets that explain the various benefits available.

They include the following:

> ***Understanding Social Security***
> (Publication No. 05–10024)
>
> ***Retirement*** (Publication No. 05–10035)
>
> ***Disability*** (Publication No. 05–1029)
>
> ***Survivors*** (Publication No. 05–10084)
>
> ***Medicare*** (Publication No. 05–10043)

A number of free worksheets are also available on specific aspects of Social Security benefits.

For a booklet, or for a complete listing of the worksheets available, call the toll-free number: 1–800–772–1213.

STEP 7

Make Your Home a Nest Egg, Not Just a Nest

Plus: Ten things you should consider before you choose a retirement home

If only we could all save for retirement the way we pay for our homes: equal payments every month for up to 30 years. That's how you pay down a mortgage, and that is *exactly* how you should save for retirement, one payment at a time.

Chances are, the two largest financial commitments you will make in your lifetime will be your home and your retirement fund. And if you play your cards right, you'll be able to use both of them to pay for your golden years.

Since World War II, the United States has been through a number of real estate booms and busts that have occurred at different times in various parts of the country. The booms occurred when demand outpaced supply, and the busts happened when speculation got out of hand.

Here is a case in point:

In 1987, my wife and I bought a ranch-style home in Southern California. Prices in the neighborhood at that time ranged from $200,000 to $300,000. But then prices took off, and within a year homes were selling for between $350,000 and $450,000.

The home directly behind us was owned by an elderly couple who had lived there for 35 years. In the fall of 1987, they sold for about $350,000.

The new owners had the house painted and re–landscaped, and by January of 1988, they had sold it again, presumably at a profit.

The next owners dug a swimming pool in the backyard, added a new fence in the front yard, and they sold the house once again by the summer of 1988.

By fall, builders came in and tore the house down, and for the next nine months they built a huge two-story mansion my wife and I dubbed the Taj Mahal.

It was completed by the summer of 1989. And guess what the owners did? Right, they put it up for sale again. Asking price: $1.6 million, more than four times what the elderly couple had sold their beloved home for just two short years earlier.

I have to admit, that got the neighborhood's attention. We watched very carefully to see how quickly the home would sell this time, knowing how much it would impact the perceived value of our homes.

Long story short: My family moved out of the neighborhood in the fall of 1991, and the Taj Mahal was still looking for a buyer. We heard later that the bank holding the mortgage foreclosed, and the house finally sold in late 1992 for something like $600,000.

It's an example of the kind of speculation that signalled the end of the real estate booms in the Northeastern part of the United States in the mid '80s and in the Southwest in the late '80s.

Speculation is fine, as long as you know what you're doing. But speculation is not appropriate for the investor saving for retirement, or for the home buyer looking for a place to put down roots.

Owning a home is, of course, the cornerstone of the American Dream. And achieving home ownership — just like achieving a comfortable retirement — takes careful planning.

How Much House Can You Afford?

Before you start shopping for a house, you should first determine how much house you can afford. You can do that by using the same two indicators your potential lender will use when he or she approves your loan application:

1) Your loan-to-value percentage.

2) Your long-term debt percentage.

Loan-to-Value Percentage

Lenders use the loan-to-value percentage to determine how much money they will loan you. It is essentially determined by the size of the down payment you're willing to make.

The loan-to-value percentage is determined by dividing the size of the loan you are seeking by the actual value of the property you are purchasing.

Loan-to-Value Ratio	
Amount of Loan	$90,000
Value of Property	$100,000
Loan-to-Value Percentage:	**90%**

In this example, the property you're purchasing is valued at $100,000, and you are willing to make a down payment of $10,000. That means the loan amount will be $90,000, or 90 percent of the value of the property.

Generally, lenders want the lowest possible loan-to-value percentage, which means they are looking for borrowers with large down payments.

Your lender will then use your loan-to-value percentage to determine the maximum monthly mortgage you can afford. If, for example, your loan-to-value percentage is 95 percent, your lender will allow your mortgage payment (that's principal and interest) to be up to 25 percent of your gross monthly income.

If your loan-to-value percentage is below 95 percent (down to, say, 80 percent), your lender could allow your mortgage payment to take up up to 38 percent of your gross monthly income. (The actual percentage is often determined by a federal agency like Federal National Mortgage Association, or "Fannie Mae." These agencies buy up hundreds of mortgages like yours, package them together, and sell them to investors. Then when you make your monthly mortgage payment, you're actually paying those investors.)

Let's assume your gross monthly income is $5,000. If your loan-to-value percentage is 90 percent, your lender will multiply $5,000 by .25 to determine the maximum monthly payment you can afford. In this case, the result is $1,250.

If your loan-to-value percentage is, say, 80 percent, your lender will multiply $5,000 by .28, which is $1,400.

(These monthly payment figures, by the way, include principal, interest, taxes, and insurance.)

Long-Term Debt Percentage

Lenders use this important indicator to decide whether they will lend you any money at all.

It is calculated by dividing *all* of your debt obligations longer than 10 months in duration (including your potential mortgage payment, any auto loans, and any lines of credit) by your gross monthly income. Your credit card balances will be considered only if they are excessive.

Long-Term Debt Percentage	
Long-Term Debt	$1,650
Gross Monthly Income	$5,000
Long-Term Debt Percentage:	**33%**

In this example, your gross monthly income is $5,000, and your long-term debt obligations (including your potential mortgage payment) are $1,650, which is 33 percent of $5,000.

Roughly speaking, if your loan-to-value percentage is 90 percent, lenders don't want your long-term debt to be any higher than 33 percent of your gross monthly income. And if your loan-to-value percentage is around 80 percent, they will allow your long-term debt to take up to 36 percent of your gross monthly income.

Table 7-1 will help you figure out the size mortgage you can afford, if you already know how much of a monthly payment you can afford.

Table 7-1

HOW MUCH MORTGAGE CAN YOU AFFORD?
The Size Mortgage You Can Afford at These Interest Rates for a 30-Year Fixed-Rate Mortgage (in $Thousands)

Your Monthly Payment	6%	6.5%	7%	7.5%	8%	8.5%	9%
$400	$67	$62	$60	$57	$55	$52	$50
$450	$75	$72	$67	$65	$62	$57	$55
$500	$82	$80	$75	$72	$70	$65	$62
$550	$92	$87	$82	$77	$75	$72	$67
$600	$100	$95	$90	$87	$82	$77	$75
$650	$109	$105	$97	$92	$87	$85	$82
$700	$115	$111	$105	$100	$95	$92	$87
$750	$125	$119	$115	$107	$102	$97	$92
$800	$135	$127	$122	$115	$110	$105	$100
$850	$145	$135	$127	$122	$115	$112	$105
$900	$150	$145	$135	$127	$122	$118	$115
$950	$157	$150	$145	$135	$130	$122	$120
$1000	$167	$160	$150	$145	$137	$130	$125
$1100	$185	$175	$157	$152	$150	$145	$135
$1200	$200	$190	$180	$172	$165	$155	$150
$1300	$220	$215	$195	$185	$177	$170	$162
$1400	$235	$222	$215	$200	$190	$185	$175
$1500	$250	$237	$225	$218	$215	$195	$185

Example: Let's assume you can afford to devote $750 a month to a mortgage payment. If the current interest rate for a 30-year fixed-rate mortgage is 7 percent, this chart shows that you could afford to secure a loan of roughly $115,000.

Understand that this chart illustrates *approximate* mortgages you could afford. The actual amount you will be able to borrow will depend on, among other things, the size of the down payment you're willing to make and the amount of debt you already have on your personal balance sheet.

Once you have determined the size mortgage you can afford, you can figure out how much money you will need to save for a down payment (usually 10–20 percent of the value of the home, plus points and closing costs).

Saving for a Down Payment

Saving for retirement should be done slowly and gradually over a few decades. It should be an integral, permanent part of your monthly budget.

Saving for the down payment on a home is different. It is a shorter-term prospect that lasts maybe three to five years. (If it takes longer than that, you're either not trying hard enough, or you can't afford the house you're trying to buy.)

Saving for a house takes careful planning and some sacrifice. To do it effectively, you should shift your monthly budget into what I call Poverty Mode.

Poverty Mode is a highly disciplined budgeting technique that emphasizes savings and eliminates unnecessary expenses.

That means:

- *No more credit card balances.* Extinguish whatever balances you have as soon as possible. This accomplishes two things: 1) It helps you focus on devoting more money to savings each month; and 2) it improves your debt ratio when the time comes to qualify for a mortgage.

- *Reduce your miscellaneous spending to a bare minimum.* This could be your biggest source of savings for the down payment. Put yourself on a strict cash and check-writing allowance.

- *Cut out "luxury" services.* No more dry cleaning, manicures, or trips to the dog groomer, for example. (That's why I call it *Poverty* Mode.)

- *No more impulse buying.* What is your weakness? Books? Shoes? Computer games? Cut them out.

- *Don't buy a new car.* Nothing eats up money in a house fund faster than a down payment for a new car. But if the old jalopy does happen to give out on you while you're in Poverty Mode, consider replacing it with an inexpensive used car. New car payments will just increase your long-term debt percentage.

- *No more dinners in restaurants.* Just before you shift into Poverty Mode, you should go out for a nice dinner, order the most expensive bottle of wine on the wine list, and drink a toast to the last dinner you'll be eating in a restaurant for a long, long time.

- *No fancy vacations.* An occasional three-day weekend may be acceptable, as long as you're not headed for Disney World, New York City, San Francisco, or some other expensive destination. Learn how to pitch a tent.

- *Wear the same clothing for another year.* You want that house, don't you?

The more disciplined you are during Poverty Mode, the less time you'll have to spend in it. Make it a fun challenge. Find out exactly how much money you are capable of saving.

To increase your resolve, put pictures of homes you like on your refrigerator or on your desk at work. Do whatever it takes to motivate yourself.

Investing Your Down-Payment Money

How you invest the money you are saving for a down payment will be determined by the amount of time you have before you plan to buy the house.

The consensus of the money managers I've interviewed over the years seems to be that if you're planning to buy a home in one or two years, you should keep your down-payment money in an interest-bearing safe haven, like a money market fund.

If you aren't planning to buy the home for three years or more, you might consider investing in a *balanced* mutual fund, which invests in equal parts blue chip stocks and high grade bonds. The idea is to give your money time to appreciate faster than the rate of inflation.

What Kind of Mortgage Should You Get?

The size of your monthly mortgage payment is determined by two factors:

- *The length, or term, of your mortgage* (in other words, the amount of time you take to pay it off).

- *The interest rate* your lender charges to loan you money.

What kind of mortgage is right for you? Let's consider the alternatives.

Fixed-Rate Versus Adjustable-Rate

Generally speaking, if you believe interest rates will be going up over the life of your mortgage, you should probably consider a fixed-rate mortgage. It will protect you from having to make higher monthly payments when interest rates rise.

Conversely, if you believe interest rates will be going down after you purchase your home, you should consider an adjustable-rate mortgage (ARM). With an ARM, your monthly payment is readjusted periodically (usually once a year) to reflect the change in interest rates. An ARM is always tied to an index.

The most common indexes are:

- *The Prime Rate.* This is the rate that banks charge their most creditworthy customers. Most lenders who tie their ARM loans to the prime rate use a composite prime rate index published in the *Wall Street Journal.*

- *Cost-of-Funds Index.* This is based on a bank's or savings and loan's own cost of borrowing money. It is compiled by the Federal Home Loan Bank Board, and it is usually reported monthly and by district. (In fact, the most commonly used cost-of-funds index comes from the FHLBB's 11th district.)

- *Treasury securities.* Some lenders determine the interest they charge for an ARM based on yields on various short-term Treasury securities, ranging from a six-month T-bill to five-year T-notes. You should be aware that the yields on these securities sometimes fluctuate quite a bit.

• *The LIBOR Rate.* This is the London Interbank Offered Rate. It is usually the lowest, most stable indicator used to determine the rates charged on ARMs.

Note: When you go with a fixed-rate mortgage, your lender assumes the interest rate risk. He or she is betting that rates won't go down too much over the life of your mortgage. And when you choose an adjustable-rate mortgage, you assume the interest rate risk because you are betting that rates won't rise appreciably over the life of your loan.

Advantages

Fixed-Rate. Your monthly payment will be predictable, remaining constant over the life of your loan.

Adjustable-Rate. Your monthly payment will usually be lower than it would be with a fixed-rate mortgage (at least in the first few years of your mortgage).

Disadvantages

Fixed-Rate. If interest rates fall dramatically after you purchase your home, you are stuck paying a higher rate, unless you decide to refinance your mortgage.

Adjustable-Rate. If interest rates rise appreciably after you purchase your home, you could eventually lose the advantage you had over the fixed-rate mortgage of making a lower monthly payment, even though ARMs traditionally include limits (or caps) on how much your rate can be raised annually and over the life of the loan. And be aware of the so-called teaser rates that most lenders offer on ARMs. These are rates that are much lower than prevailing market rates, and they don't accurately reflect what your actual mortgage payment will be. Teaser rates are usually only good for the first six months of your mortgage.

Generally speaking, ARMs work best for people who plan to own a home for less than, say, five years. If you plan to stay in your home longer, especially for the duration of your mortgage, a fixed-rate mortgage might be the better way to go. If rates decline, you can always refinance. (More about that later in the chapter.)

If you aren't sure how long you will own your home, you might consider some of the new kinds of mortgages available now.

Here are two typical examples:

- One kind of adjustable-rate mortgage adjusts the interest rate charged every three years. This allows the borrower to lock in an adjustable-rate for a longer period of time.

- Another kind of mortgage begins with a fixed-rate that lasts for five to seven years, and then the interest rate is adjusted annually for the duration of the loan.

15-Year Versus 30-Year Mortgages

Do you want a low monthly payment, or do you want to quickly build up equity in your home? Your decision will help you figure out whether you want a 30-year mortgage or a 15-year mortgage.

The 30-year mortgage was developed to help a borrower afford a home by stretching payments out over a long enough period of time to make the payments small and, therefore, affordable.

The hidden disadvantage of a 30-year mortgage is that the borrower ends up paying the lender much more than the stated amount of the loan. For example, on a $100,000 30-year fixed-rate mortgage with a 7 percent interest rate, after 30 years the borrower will actually have paid the lender a total of $239,511.60. And that doesn't include the points and fees paid when the loan was made.

A 15-year mortgage allows the borrower to pay off a home loan in half the time it takes to pay off a 30-year mortgage. One disadvantage is the monthly payment for a 15-year mortgage is larger than it is for a 30-year mortgage for the same loan amount. For example, the $100,000 30-year mortgage with the 7 percent interest rate I mentioned before carries a monthly payment of $665.31. The monthly payment for a 15-year mortgage on the same loan would be $898.83.

But the 15-year mortgage has at least two advantages over the 30-year mortgage:

- *The borrower ends up paying the lender a lot less* over the life of the loan. With our $100,000 loan at 7 percent, a 15-year mortgage means the borrower pays the lender a total of $161,789.40 (or $77,722.20 less than you would have paid over the life of a comparable 30-year mortgage).

- *Equity builds up in the home a lot faster.* Table 7-2 shows you exactly how much faster.

Table 7-2

EQUITY ACCUMULATION
($100,000 30-year fixed-rate mortgage with a 7 percent interest rate)

	After 5 Years	After 10 Years
15-year mortgage	$22,587	$54,607
30-year mortgage	$5,868	$14,187

With a 30-year mortgage, after 15 years the borrower has paid off only slightly more than 25 percent of the loan. It is not until the 22nd year of the loan (or 3/4 of the loan's life) that half the loan is actually paid.

With a 15-year mortgage, half of the loan is paid off in the ninth year.

Variations on the 15-year mortgage. If you are currently paying off a 30-year mortgage, you can still pay it off without having to refinance to a 15-year mortgage. Here are two ways.

Make an extra principal payment each month. Your monthly mortgage payment is made up of two components: principal and interest.

Note: *Your lender may also include mortgage insurance and property taxes in your payment.*

The principal portion pays down a tiny fraction of the actual loan amount, and the interest portion is what you pay your lender each month to carry the balance of your loan. (Your lender will be able to tell you the exact breakdown of principal and interest in your monthly payment.)

In order to pay your mortgage off in half the time, write a separate check to your lender each month for the amount equal to the principal portion of your mortgage payment. Label the check "principal only." This will reduce your loan amount twice as fast.

Note: *Some lenders make it easy by including a space on payment coupons for itemizing a principal-only payment.*

Make an extra mortgage payment each year. Instead of making an extra, principal-only payment each month, you can make a 13th mortgage payment each year. (Be sure to mark your check "principal only.") This one extra mortgage payment each year will enable you to pay off your 30-year mortgage in about 22 years.

When Should You Refinance?

The rule of thumb used to be that you wouldn't think about refinancing your mortgage until rates fell two full percentage points below the rate you were currently paying. And then it would only make sense to refinance if you planned to stay in the house long enough to off-set the new loan's up-front costs with the amount you would be saving on your new monthly mortgage payment (which usually took up to two years).

All of that changed, though, a few years ago when lenders started offering refinance packages with no up-front costs. (What they did was add all costs to the amount of the new loan.)

The interest rate on a no-cost re-finance package will always be higher than the rate offered on a conventional refinance package. So if you're planning to stay in your home longer than, say, five years, you might consider going with the conventional package with the lower interest rate, even though the no-cost package is very tempting.

Don't forget, every time you refinance your mortgage, the payment clock starts all over again. If, for example, you've been in your home for seven years, and you refinance your existing 30-year fixed-rate mortgage with another 30-year fixed-rate mortgage, you are essentially adding another seven years of mortgage payments to your monthly budget.

You should also realize that when you refinance your mortgage to a lower interest rate, you are losing some tax benefits since mortgage interest is one of the few deductions left to taxpayers. You might consult a tax expert before you refinance to make sure the benefits of lower interest costs aren't outweighed by the reduced tax deductions.

"They spent years paying for their home. Why couldn't their home pay them back?"

Reverse Mortgages

For years, the great irony about home ownership was that retired people, living a painfully frugal lifestyle on a fixed income, sometimes lived in big expensive homes. And they couldn't tap the equity in their most valuable — and beloved — asset unless they sold it, which they were loathe to do. A survey released in 1992 by the American Association of Retired Persons (AARP) found that a whopping 84 percent of older Americans planned to stay in their homes the rest of their lives.

They spent years paying for their home. Why couldn't their home pay them back?

That is what a reverse mortgage is all about. This is where you can turn your nest into a nest egg.

When you take out a reverse mortgage, you borrow money from a lender and promise to pay it back — with interest — when your house is sold.

Reverse mortgages have been around since 1961, when they were originally offered to elderly homeowners who couldn't afford to pay property taxes or to cover normal home repairs on their fixed incomes.

But they didn't really catch on until the late '80s when the government got involved and offered to insure them.

Today, you can choose an adjustable-rate reverse mortgage insured by the Federal Housing Administration (FHA) or an adjustable or fixed-rate reverse mortgage insured by a private lender.

The amount of money you are paid by a reverse mortgage is determined by three things:

1) Your age. Lenders generally don't offer reverse mortgages to anyone under age 62. And the older the borrower, the more money they will receive.

2) The amount of equity you have in your home. When you secure an FHA insured reverse mortgage, there is a cap on the amount of equity that you can tap in your home. It ranges from $67,500 in rural areas of the country where home prices are generally lower than the national average, up to $151,725 in more expensive metropolitan areas. Privately insured reverse mortgages generally have higher, negotiable, equity loan caps.

3) The kind of reverse mortgage you choose. There are five kinds:

- A line of credit that allows you to withdraw only what you need, when you need it.

- The so-called "term" option, which pays the borrower a series of fixed monthly payments for a predetermined period of time, usually 10 years. (You should be aware that at the end of the time period, the borrower must immediately begin to repay the loan.)

- The so-called "tenure" option, which provides borrowers with a monthly check for as long as they occupy the house.

- A line of credit coupled with a "term" type of reverse mortgage.

- A line of credit coupled with a "tenure" type of reverse mortgage.

Tables 7-3 and 7-4 give you an idea of the kind of monthly payment a borrower could expect from an FHA-insured reverse mortgage.

Table 7-3

MONTHLY PAYMENTS FOR 10-YEAR TERM REVERSE MORTGAGE			
Borrower's Age	Amount of Home Equity		
	$50,000	**$75,000**	**$100,000**
65	$146	$262	$378
75	$233	$391	$549
85	$340	$547	$755
source: FNMA			

Table 7-4

MONTHLY PAYMENTS FOR TENURE REVERSE MORTGAGE			
Borrower's Age	Amount of Home Equity		
	$50,000	**$75,000**	**$100,000**
65	$90	$162	$234
75	$154	$259	$364
85	$272	$438	$604
source: FNMA			

Because of the fees involved, a reverse mortgage is cost effective only for people who plan to be in their homes for a minimum of five years. It makes much more sense for people who plan to be in their homes for at least 10 years.

If you don't think you'll be in your home that long, and you still need additional monthly income, TransAmerica HomeFirst offers a kind of *portable* reverse mortgage that will continue to pay you a monthly income even after you have sold your home. (Essentially, it is an annuity tied to your home equity.)

The company charges a $15,000 one-time premium that is deducted from the proceeds when you sell your home.

Who to Call

Federal National Mortgage Association (Fannie Mae) has a pamphlet, free of charge, that describes how an FHA insured reverse mortgage works. It also includes a list of FHA insured lenders who offer reverse mortgages. Call: 1 (800) 7–FANNIE.

The American Association of Retired Persons (AARP) also offers a list of reverse mortgage lenders.

Call: (800) 434–6066.

For more information about TransAmerica HomeFirst's portable reverse mortgage, call (800) 538–5569.

Choosing a Retirement Home

I'm only going to make one prediction in this book, and here it is: The next Great Real Estate Boom our country experiences will occur when the Baby Boomer generation gets ready to retire. It will begin as a trickle in the year 2000 when the vanguard of the generation hits age 55. But the full effect won't be felt until 2020 when the bulk of the generation has hit retirement age.

The boom will occur in the so-called Sun Belt portion of the country, for obvious reasons. And the biggest demand will be for small, low-priced housing, like condominiums and mobile homes, for three reasons:

1) *A good portion of the members of the generation will find themselves cutting corners* in their budgets because they didn't save enough to retire on.

2) *The equity they get out of the homes they owned during their working days won't be enough* to buy a new home *and* provide some retirement income. First, because I don't believe home values will appreciate in the next 20–30 years nearly as much as they did the past 20–30 years. And second, because — unlike previous generations who stayed in one place a long time and paid their mortgages off — more than a few highly mobile Boomers will still be making mortgage payments when they retire.

3) *A number of Boomers waited to start families* until they were in their mid to late 30s, so about the time they are serious about saving for retirement they will also be helping their children pay for college.

Ten Things You Should Consider Before You Choose a Retirement Home

When the time does arrive to think about retiring, here are 10 things you should look for in a retirement community:

1) An agreeable climate.

2) An affordable cost of living: housing, property, and local income taxes, etc.

3) Access to quality medical care.

4) Proximity to major highways and airports.

5) A low crime rate.

6) A relatively stable housing market in case you decide to sell.

7) An abundance of activities that interest you: cultural, athletic, etc.

8) Enough business and education opportunities in the area in case you decide to work part time or go back to school.

9) Proximity to commerce: shopping, services, etc.

10) Proximity to friends and family. Don't completely cut yourself off from your network of significant others immediately after you retire. If you want to get away from it all, take a long vacation first.

STEP 8

Let Insurance Be Your Prosperity's Safety Net

Don't play "chicken" with disaster

The images on the CNBC studio monitors were hard to believe that day in early 1994. We were showing pictures of homes and businesses that had been damaged, of highways that had been destroyed, and I was on the air reporting that hundreds, maybe thousands, of residents were homeless.

I thought about other pictures we had televised in 1992 of the devastation caused by Hurricane Andrew in Florida, Louisiana, and elsewhere, and of the pictures in the summer of 1993 of the worst floods in 500 years, floods that changed thousands of people's lives in the Midwest.

But this time was different. This time I was talking about the devastating 6.6 earthquake that rocked Southern California before dawn on January 17, 1994. It was centered in the town of Northridge. My hometown.

It was incredibly eerie, seeing pictures of burning buildings on the campus of my wife's and my alma mater, California State University, Northridge. And of the collapsed buildings and parking structure at the huge Northridge Mall, where I had worked in college.

At one point, a producer informed me that we would be showing pictures of a supermarket where people were lined up outside waiting to buy water. When the pictures came up on the screen, I was shocked to see the market where my wife and I used to do our shopping.

"Insurance is complicated. But it is very, very important. And it provides a measure of control over your financial future that is critical to achieving financial prosperity."

The first person we heard from in the quake area that morning was my wife's sister. She and her family had a magnificent home on a hill overlooking the whole San Fernando Valley, and it had sustained major damage. Thankfully, no one was seriously hurt, but the home was going to have to be rebuilt. One of the last things her sister said to us before we hung up the phone was, "Thank God I decided to renew the earthquake insurance."

Indeed. Insurance is one of the few products you buy that you hope you will never have to use. People who don't buy it are playing "chicken" with disaster.

Insurance is complicated. But it is very, very important. And it provides a measure of control over your financial future that is critical to achieving financial prosperity. No matter how large or small your nest egg is, you could lose it all if

- *A crippling injury* cuts off your income and drains your savings.

- *A natural disaster* wipes out your home and all of your belongings.

- *A lawsuit* results in a judgment against you that is larger than your total net worth.

Chances are, none of that will happen to you. But what if it does? Would the members of your family have to drastically reduce their standard of living if you died in an auto accident tomorrow? (assuming you provided a major source of income). Would you still be able to pay your bills if you were unable to work for six months because of a severe injury?

You need to answer two questions *before* you buy any kind of insurance:

- What are my insurance needs?
- What types of policies will best meet those needs?

I'm not here to sell you insurance. But if you're going to work hard to save money for your retirement and/or your child's college education, your job is not complete until you have *insured* the safety of that money.

Let's review the types of insurance you may need.

Life Insurance

Who Needs It?

Generally, married people with a family need life insurance. So do single people with relatives or friends who depend on their income.

But don't buy too much. Life insurance should be viewed merely as income replacement in the event of your death. It is not necessary to turn your dependents into instant millionaires when you die. It is certainly a noble thought, but you'll end up in the poor house just paying the premiums.

How Much Should I Buy?

The general rule of thumb is to buy life insurance that represents five times your annual salary. If you make $50,000 a year, for example, you probably will want to buy a $250,000 policy.

What Kind Should I Buy?

It depends entirely on you. Let's examine the different kinds of life insurance:

Term

This is the simplest, cheapest, and purest kind of life insurance you can buy. You buy it for a specified period of time (typically one year, five years, or even 10 years at a time), pay your premium once or twice a year, and when you die the insurance company pays your beneficiaries the death benefit outlined in your policy.

Advantage:

- *It is relatively inexpensive.* You generally get more insurance for your money than you do with other kinds of life insurance.

Disadvantages:

- *Premiums automatically rise as you get older,* especially as you approach retirement age.

- *Renewing your policy can become difficult,* if not impossible, if you develop a serious medical condition.

Cash Value

The problem some people have with term life insurance is they — the policyholders — never realize any benefits themselves. For years, they pay money to an insurance company, and then they die. Plus, as I said before, premiums become quite high as the policyholder approaches retirement age. Paying for term insurance eats into a retired person's fixed income.

So in the 1960s, insurance companies started introducing products that not only paid death benefits, but also accumulated a cash value that served two purposes: 1) It allowed a policyholder to derive a financial benefit while he or she was still alive by either borrowing from the policy's cash account or deriving monthly income from it via an annuity, and 2) The cash portion of the policy helped reduce the premiums.

Today, there are generally three kinds of cash-value life insurance policies available: whole life, universal life, and variable life.

Whole life: This is the granddaddy of cash-value policies. A portion of a policyholder's premium covers the insurance company's costs, and the rest is invested in things like stocks and bonds. Whole life policies pay dividends, which the policyholder can either receive, reinvest, or use to pay future premiums.

Policyholders can also borrow up to 95 percent of the accumulated cash value of the policy. (If the policyholder dies before the loan is repaid, the unpaid portion is simply deducted from the death benefit.)

Policyholders can also choose to "annuitize" the cash portion of their policy and start receiving a guaranteed monthly income for life. The size of the monthly check will be determined by the amount of money accumulated in the policy.

Universal life: Universal life policies are unusually flexible. They allow policyholders to essentially set the level and frequency of premiums they pay (although certain minimum levels must be met). Policyholders can also adjust the amount of coverage they receive as their needs change through the years.

Universal life policies invest in short-term debt obligations. As a result, their rate of return is usually reset annually. They were very popular in the early '80s when interest rates were quite high. But their popularity has waned in the low interest rate environment of the '90s.

Variable life: This is the insurance industry's answer to mutual funds. The cash portion of a variable life policy is invested in a group of *subaccounts*, which are essentially mutual funds with varying degrees of risk and investment objectives, managed by either the insurance company or an outside money management company. As with many mutual fund families, variable life policyholders can shift the cash portion of their policy among the various subaccounts offered as market conditions change.

Advantages:

- *The money earned by cash-value life insurance policies is tax deferred:* You do not pay taxes on the money earned in the account until you withdraw it.

- *Cash-value policies can be a good way to save money* for retirement, especially variable life policies.

- *Cash-value policies can be cheaper than term policies in the long run,* since term policy premiums rise as the policyholder ages, and the cash portion of the cash-value policies can be used to pay policy premiums.

Disadvantages:

- *There are a number of fees involved with cash-value policies.* After all, you're paying for life insurance *and* money management. If, for example, you find that you must withdraw the money accumulated in a cash-value policy, you will be assessed a surrender penalty by the insurance company if you have held the policy fewer than, say, seven or eight years. Also, if you're younger than 59 1/2, the IRS also requires you to pay a stiff 10 percent tax on any earned income. (The 10 percent penalty does *not* apply if you decide to annuitize the cash built up in the policy and receive it as monthly income.)

Group Life Insurance Plans

This is life insurance offered to employees of large corporations. The company usually pays the premium. And the policy normally covers up to twice your annual salary.

Advantage:

- Companies often allow employees to buy additional life insurance at the same discounted premiums. This is a great way to buy insurance. (After all, you're getting a group rate!)

Disadvantage:

- If you leave the company, your policy is usually canceled on the next renewal date.

Okay, So What Kind of Life Insurance Should I Buy?

Here are some suggestions.

Term: This is the insurance to buy if 1) all you want is life insurance and 2) you are a disciplined saver already making regular contributions to a retirement account.

Whole life: If you are not a very disciplined saver, you might consider this kind of policy since part of your premium is invested in a savings account with a guaranteed (but very modest) rate of return that is tax deferred. If you consider yourself a conservative investor, this is probably for you.

Variable life: If you are not a very disciplined saver, and you are willing to take more risk, this insurance-policy-attached-to-a-mutual-fund might be for you, especially since the money earned by the policy's investments is tax deferred.

Universal life: If you are not a very disciplined saver, and you want 1) a higher return than a whole life policy provides and 2) less risk than a variable life policy offers, you might consider this kind of policy. The money earned by the policy is also tax deferred. But remember: universal life policies are relatively expensive, and they don't offer much of a return when interest rates are low.

Group plans: If you work for a large corporation that offers group plans, this is probably the best way to go. But remember: your coverage usually ends if you leave the company.

Annuities

Simply put, an annuity is an investment you make through an insurance company that will either *immediately* or *eventually* provide you with a certain amount of income. You might think of an annuity as *income insurance.*

You could always invest your money in a bank CD or in stock and bond mutual funds. In fact, an annuity does that for you, and — unlike CDs or mutual funds — your money grows on a *tax-deferred* basis. You do not have to declare income earned in an annuity to the IRS until you begin to withdraw the money.

> *"Simply put, an annuity is an investment you make through an insurance company that will either immediately or eventually provide you with a certain amount of income."*

There are basically two types of annuities: *immediate*, and *deferred*.

Immediate

This is for people who want income immediately. The size of your monthly check will be determined by how much money you have to begin with and how long you want the payments to last.

Deferred

Deferred annuities are for people who have a number of years to go before retirement. You set up a regular schedule of contributions into the account, and then when you retire, you set up a regular schedule of payments.

How do you want the money in your annuity to be invested? You can go one of two ways: fixed-rate annuities, or variable-rate annuities.

Fixed-rate annuities: A fixed-rate annuity is an insurance company's version of a bank CD. It invests your money in an interest-bearing security that guarantees a certain rate of return.

And, as with CDs, insurance companies offer varying lengths of maturity. The longer the maturity, the higher the guaranteed rate of return. Lengths of maturity are usually in the one- to five-year range; you can roll them over after that.

Variable-rate annuities: The variable-rate annuity is the insurance company's answer to a family of mutual funds. And because your money grows tax free, they have become extremely popular with mutual fund investors. Variable annuities took in $20 billion in 1992 and another $40 billion in 1993.

Variable annuities offer a menu of investments to choose from called *subaccounts*. Essentially, they are mutual funds with varying degrees of risk. (See Chapter 4 for more information on mutual funds.)

There are a few charges you should know about when it comes to variable-rate annuities.

Contract charges: These are often annual fees you pay that can be fixed ($35–$50), or else they represent a percentage of the value of your annuity (usually .5 to 1.5 percent).

Subaccount charges: These are the fees paid to the mutual funds your annuity is invested in. They are usually less than the fees normally charged by mutual funds, because annuity money is not deposited and withdrawn with the same frequency.

Surrender penalty: You will be charged a surrender penalty if you make an early, unscheduled withdrawal from your annuity. The amount of the surrender penalty declines over time. If you leave your money in the annuity for seven to eight years, the surrender penalty eventually disappears.

A key to success with variable annuities is investing for the long term. All of the fees and charges involved with annuities tend to eat up any early investment gains. Over time, though, as the fees and charges are reduced, any gains are free to grow at a more rapid clip.

When Should I Consider Buying an Annuity?

Let's go over some typical situations.

Retirement: This is the most obvious use for annuities. You are not limited on the amount of money you can invest in an annuity annually, unlike 401(k)s or individual retirement accounts. (The big difference, though, is you invest *pre-tax* dollars in qualified retirement accounts, while you invest *after-tax* dollars in annuities.)

And don't forget, in order to overcome the effect of the many fees and charges related to annuities, it is best to invest in annuities for the long haul.

College: You might consider putting money into an annuity that is designed to begin paying off when your children, or grandchildren, start college. (See Chapter 10 for a more thorough discussion of how to save for your child's college education.)

Disabled dependents: A friend of mine who has a mentally handicapped daughter bought an annuity that will begin paying his daughter's living expenses when she reaches adulthood. It serves two purposes: 1) It reduces his financial burden when he and his wife start living on a fixed income at retirement, and 2) It continues to provide for their daughter if something happens to him and/or his wife.

Lottery winner: Okay, so this isn't very typical. But if you should hit The Big One, and you don't know a whole lot about handling that much money, you might consider buying an annuity that provides you with a monthly check. (As they say in the commercials for the New York state lottery: "Hey, you never know.")

Note: At the end of this chapter, I list the ten largest variable annuities on the market right now.

Disability Insurance

Insurance company research shows that by the age of 30, you have about a 50–50 chance of being physically disabled for up to three months before you reach age 65. If you aren't one of those thrifty types who keeps six months' salary in an accessible interest-bearing account at all times, you might look into disability insurance in order to avert financial disaster.

"Make sure the private policy will pay off even if you already have an employer-sponsored policy."

Some employers often pay for a modest amount, covering a percentage of your salary (usually 50–60 percent) during the period you are disabled. But you might also consider buying additional private disability insurance to give you more complete coverage.

One caveat: Make sure the private policy will pay off even if you already have an employer-sponsored policy. Some private policies don't allow you to recoup more than 80 percent of your salary even when other policies are involved.

Yes, you can qualify for *Worker's Compensation insurance,* but there are some restrictions. For example, it only covers you when you injure yourself at work. It does not cover any accidents you may have at home. And Worker's Compensation generally covers only 60 percent of your lost wages.

Social Security also provides disability income, but you must have been employed for 5 of the previous 10 years, and you must be disabled for at least 12 months before you can begin collecting.

Because of all of the variables involved in disability insurance, you really have to do your homework before you sign up for any policy. There are three main questions you need to ask your insurance agent.

How does the policy define "disability"?

This is very important. For example, does the policy say that you must be completely disabled in order to collect, or can you collect if your disability merely prohibits you from performing the duties of your job? Some policies will not pay off if you're physically able to do some other kind of work in the same profession.

What is the policy's "waiting period"?

The waiting period is measured from the time you initially become disabled until the insurance company begins to pay you benefits. You should know that the longer the waiting period is, the cheaper the insurance coverage will be.

If you have enough savings in the bank to pay your monthly expenses for, say, three months, you might consider a disability policy with a three-month waiting period. If you can wait six months before the insurance company has to pay off, your premiums will be even lower.

What is the policy's "benefit period"?

The benefit period is the time during which the insurance company is paying you to cover your lost wages. Disability policies generally come with one of two benefit periods.

Short-term: These are designed to replace lost income for periods of disability up to one year.

Long-term: These policies are designed for periods longer than one year. Depending on the policy, the insurance company might pay you until you reach age 65 (when other benefits typically kick in), or if your disability is serious enough, it might pay you for the rest of your life.

Umbrella Insurance

Just when you thought you had enough auto or homeowner's insurance, disaster strikes:

- *You are sued* for your role in an automobile accident, you lose, and the final judgment exceeds your auto insurance coverage.

- *Someone has an accident in your home*, sues you, and wins a huge judgment.

Enter: *umbrella insurance*, also known as *excess liability* or *personal catastrophe insurance*. These policies provide you with coverage above and beyond the liability coverage your auto and/or homeowner policies afford. Umbrella policies can be written for coverage of anywhere between $1,000,000 and $5,000,000. And, because of the low probability that you will ever need it, premiums are typically very, very low (usually somewhere around $100–$150 annually for $1,000,000 of coverage).

In order to buy umbrella insurance, though, you must already have a minimum amount of liability coverage on your auto and homeowner policies.

Health Insurance

This is easily the most important type of insurance you can have. It is also the most confusing. The health insurance industry in our country is going through a major transition. And for good reason. The system is out of control.

The paperwork involved is often voluminous and unnecessary. Some doctors won't take certain patients because they have the wrong kind of insurance. Some patients won't go to certain doctors because their insurance policies won't pay for the visit, even if they could afford to pay for the visit out of their own pocket. And drug pricing is out of control. Generic versions of some drugs sometimes cost less than half what you pay for the identical, patented version.

But the system is changing quickly. Drug manufacturers have started holding the line on price increases.

Large, healthy medical care providers have begun buying up smaller, financially troubled providers and turning them around. Even insurance companies have been exploring ways to standardize (and simplify!) paperwork. And, of course, the federal government is planning to reform the whole health care system.

Your best defense as a consumer is to fully understand how the health care industry works, to pay attention to all the changes occurring right now, and to know what your options are as a consumer and a patient.

"Your best defense as a consumer is to fully understand how the health care industry works, to pay attention to all the changes occurring right now, and to know what your options are as a consumer and a patient."

Let's go over the basics of health insurance.

There are generally three kinds of health insurance in this country:

- Fee-for-service plans.
- Prepaid plans.
- Medicare.

Fee-for-Service Plans

Under this type of plan, your doctor deals directly with your insurance company. You don't get involved in the paperwork. The one drawback of these plans is you often don't get to use your own doctor. Instead, you choose from a list provided by the insurance company. (Blue Cross and Blue Shield are good examples of fee-for-service medical providers.)

There are generally five kinds of fee-for-service medical plans to choose from: hospital expense, surgical expense, general medical expense, major medical, and comprehensive medical.

Hospital expense: This plan covers most of the expenses you incur during a hospital stay.

Surgical expense: This covers the cost of surgery, minus any deductible.

General medical expense: This covers the cost of office visits, again minus any applicable deductible.

Major medical: This essentially combines the coverage offered under hospital, surgical, and general medical expense plans. This is the type of plan often offered by smaller employers, and it is the type of plan you should buy if you are out of work or self-employed.

There are three important features you should be familiar with when it comes to major medical coverage.

Deductibles: Obviously, the more you are willing to pay out of pocket for medical treatment, the smaller your insurance premium will be. If you feel you have saved enough money in a reserve account to handle periodic medical expenses, look into raising your deductibles in order to save money on premiums.

Coinsurance: Insurance companies will ask you to pay a percentage of what they call "eligible expenses" beyond your deductible. This feature can be quite confusing. You may think your only liability is your deductible. But that is not always true.

For example, let's say your major medical insurance plan includes a 10 percent coinsurance feature in addition to your $250 deductible. If you're involved in an accident, and you run up a $1,000 medical bill, you could be liable for up to $325 of the total bill ($250 for your deductible, and 10 percent of the remaining $750, or $75).

Stop-loss limit: Most major medical plans will only enforce the coinsurance feature up to a certain amount, usually $10,000. If your medical bill exceeds that amount, most insurance companies will pay 100 percent of the bill above $10,000.

Comprehensive Medical: This includes major medical coverage plus dental and optical coverage. It often covers treatment for alcohol and drug addiction and cosmetic surgery. And lately, some comprehensive medical plans have started to cover treatment by practitioners like chiropractors, podiatrists, and psychologists.

This is the type of plan offered by major corporations. Employees are usually offered two levels of coverage:

Basic Coverage: This covers most expenses involving hospital, surgical, and physician care, minus any deductible you are asked to pay.

The insurance company will sometimes impose a negotiable dollar limit on care (usually involving surgical and physician care) and a negotiable time limit on hospital stays.

Major medical coverage: It is designed to pick up where basic coverage leaves off, paying a higher percentage for a more extensive menu of medical care.

This is usually the best value in health insurance coverage, because it offers bargain basement premiums and deductibles in exchange for a higher volume of business offered by major corporations.

This kind of coverage would be prohibitively expensive for individuals to pay for.

Prepaid Medical Coverage

This is the kind of medical care provided by health maintenance organizations (HMOs), which act as both insurer and medical care provider.

HMO members pay a fixed monthly premium, and in turn they receive all of the medical care they need without further charge.

The advantage here is a patient receives inexpensive comprehensive medical care. The disadvantage is the care is often impersonal. A patient rarely sees the same doctor twice, given the "assembly line" nature of most HMOs.

But make no mistake about it. Prepaid health coverage is the wave of the future. Even major corporations that already offer comprehensive fee-for-service plans to employees are required by the federal government to offer prepaid plans as alternatives.

Medicare

This is the medical insurance plan offered to people age 65 and over and to people who are disabled.

There are two types of Medicare coverage:

Hospital: This is also referred to as Part A coverage. It helps pay for inpatient hospital care and some follow-up services. This service is free to all retired and/or disabled persons who are eligible for Social Security benefits. (See Chapter 5 for a more thorough discussion of Social Security eligibility requirements.)

Medical: This is optional coverage, also referred to as Part B coverage. It helps pay for doctors' services, out-patient hospital care, and other medical services. It is not free, though. Premiums usually run about $36 a month.

The Future of Health Insurance

No one knows what health insurance coverage will be like in 20 to 30 years. Will fee-for-service coverage survive, or will prepaid HMO plans prevail?

And will Medicare eventually be phased out in favor of prepaid plans that will be designed to cover us from cradle to grave?

At this point, there are many more questions than answers.

Summary

Insurance is an unpleasant necessity.

Life insurance: If you are married with children, or if you are single and other people depend on your income, you should definitely have some life insurance (usually an amount equal to five times your annual salary).

Disability insurance: If you haven't saved an amount of money equal to six months of your salary, and your employer doesn't provide you with a policy that pays more than 60 percent of your wages if you are disabled, you should look into buying some form of disability insurance.

Umbrella insurance: If your job requires you to drive a lot, or if you work at home and receive clients there, you should consider umbrella insurance to augment your basic auto and homeowner's insurance.

Annuities: If you 1) face certain circumstances in the future that could be a drain on your income (expensive college tuition or care of a disabled relative), or if 2) you're looking for a vehicle that provides a certain level of guaranteed income for a guaranteed period of time, you should consider buying an annuity through an insurance company.

Health insurance: This is the most rapidly changing form of insurance coverage. Pay close attention to developments as health insurance reform proposals slowly make their way through Congress.

Right now, consumers don't have a lot of health care plans to choose from. They are often limited to what an employer has to offer.

That may, or may not, change with health care reform.

Who to Call

When you're in the market for insurance, start by calling one or two agents. Ask for brochures, or set up meetings. Ask plenty of questions, make sure each agent fully understands your needs and how much you can afford, and make sure you understand everything about a policy before you sign on the dotted line.

If you are thinking about annuities, here is a list of the ten largest variable annuities in the country (as of 12/31/93) to help you get started.

TEN LARGEST VARIABLE ANNUITY CONTRACTS
AS OF 12/31/93

Total Assets in Billions	Policy Name	Total Assets in Billions	Policy Name
58.76	**TIAA-CREF** 730 Third Ave. New York, NY 10017 800–842–2733	4.08	**Hartford Director** P.O. Box 2999 Hartford, CT 06104 800–862–6668
7.12	**IDS Flexible Annuity** IDS Tower 10 Minneapolis, MN 55440 800–437–0401	3.92	**Equitable EQUI-VEST** P.O. Box 2996 New York, NY 10116 800–628–6673
6.04	**Lincoln Natl American Legacy II** P.O. Box 2340 Fort Wayne, IN 46801 800–421–9900	3.90	**Best of America IV/Nationwide** P.O. Box 16609 One Nationwide Plaza Columbus, OH 43216 800–243–6295
4.57	**Franklin Valuemark II** 10 Valley Stream Pky. Malvern, PA 19355 800–342–3863	3.38	**Aetna VA Acct C** 151 Farmington Ave. Hartford, CT 06156 800–262–3862
4.40	**Hartford Putnam Capital Manager** P.O. Box 2999 Hartford, CT 06104 800–354–4000	2.74	**Prudential Discovery Plus** Prudential Plaza Newark, NJ 07102 201–802–6000

STEP 9

Make Your Estate Planning Fun
Yes, you need a will! (And maybe a living trust, too)

What would you say if I told you that there was an obscure law in the United States that says a last will and testament does not become valid until the person who wrote it is either retired or on his or her death bed?

You would say that that sounds ridiculous, and you would be right. No such law exists.

So why do most of us act as if it did? Statistics show that the vast majority of all people in this country die without a will. What does that mean? It means we allow complete strangers to decide who gets all of our stuff when we die.

So why do so few people get around to drawing up a will?

"I'm not old enough."

How old is "old enough"?

Don't think of a will as a "last will and testament." It is merely a description of the things you own, coupled with a list of the people who will get those things when you die.

"I don't have enough assets to warrant a will."

Actually, the size of your estate has little to do with the need for a will. Whether your only worldly possession is a favorite coffee mug or the entire coffee mug factory, chances are you need a will.

"As long as your will is drawn up properly and signed by three witnesses (who, by the way, are not beneficiaries of your will), a probate judge has to follow your wishes to the letter."

If you are married and have children, you definitely need a will. Even if you are single and you don't have any dependents, it is still a good idea to have a legal document outlining what you want done with your assets when you die.

"I don't know how to draw up a will."

As long as you follow a few simple procedures to make sure it is legal, creating a will is not all that difficult.

Let's go over the basics.

What Is a Will?

A will is a document that outlines how you want your assets distributed when you die. And if you have children, your will identifies who you want to take custody of them if you and your spouse die at the same time.

As long as your will is drawn up properly and signed by three witnesses (who, by the way, are *not* beneficiaries of your will), a probate judge has to follow your wishes to the letter.

What Happens If I Die without a Will?

If you die without a will, our legal system says you died *intestate*. Dying intestate means your estate will be divided according to the laws of the state in which you were living when you died. The courts will appoint a state employee to oversee the disposition of your assets. (Chances are, your favorite coffee mug won't go where you wanted it to.)

If you and your spouse die at the same time and you leave behind children who are still minors, state officials will decide who cares for them. And they may, or may not, choose the custodians you would have chosen.

"Simply put, dying without a will is a dumb idea."

Simply put, dying without a will is a dumb idea.

Do I Need an Attorney to Draw Up My Will?

Yes and no.

Yes if you're talking about a rather complicated estate: a number of assets, a number of beneficiaries, a number of contingencies (such as: "If person A precedes me in death, then my coffee mug will go to person C.").

No you may not need an attorney if you're not talking about a very complicated estate. If it is pretty clear who is going to get what (everything, for example, goes to your spouse or to your only child), then you can probably draw up the will yourself. But keep in mind there are certain customary guidelines you should follow. (And if you're aren't completely sure about the whole process, by all means check with an attorney who specializes in estate planning.)

Okay, So What Do I Put in a Will?

Executor

You must name an executor. This is the person who will *execute* what you have outlined in your will. If you are married, it is customary to name your spouse as your executor, but you don't have to.

You should probably name an alternate executor in case your first choice is unable to carry out the duties for whatever reason. (**Hint:** Before you name someone as your executor, ask ahead of time if he or she will agree to do it.)

You should also include how much money or property, if any, you are leaving your executor as compensation for his or her effort.

Property

You should provide a thorough description of the property you own. (Don't forget to include your life insurance policy or policies.) Be sure to identify all of your *liabilities* (such as a mortgage) and *obligations* (contractual or otherwise), because they will have to be satisfied upon your death.

Beneficiaries

Identify your dependents and/or others you plan to leave something to. You should be as thorough and clear as possible here. Nothing should be assumed.

Note: If you are married, the state you live in determines how explicit you should be in leaving things in your will to your spouse:

Eight states are considered *community property* states. They are: Arizona, California, Idaho, Nevada, New Mexico, Texas, Washington, and Wisconsin. In these states, the law says that whatever assets you accumulate during your marriage belong equally to you and your spouse. So it is not necessary to explicitly bequeath these assets to your spouse. Listing them as joint assets will be enough. You *must*, however, specifically bequeath anything you may have personally inherited during your marriage. That is not considered community property.

All other states are considered *common law* states. The laws in those states can vary a great deal. But, generally speaking, if you die without a will and leave a spouse with no children, it is assumed that your spouse will get everything. If you leave a spouse and, say, two children, then each of them will automatically inherit a third of your estate, *unless your will says otherwise.*

Domicile

Domicile is taken from the Latin word *domicilium,* meaning "abode." You must identify the state you live in in order to determine the laws that will govern the execution of your will. This seems obvious, but given the differences between community property states and common law states (not to mention the different estate tax laws in each state), it is a good idea to specifically identify your state of residence. For the record, in case you have homes in two different states, your home state is determined by where you are registered to vote.

Attestation clause

At the end of your will, you must *attest* to the fact that 1) you knew what you were doing when you wrote the will ("being of sound mind and body," etc.) and 2) you were not coerced into writing the will.

Signature

You must sign your will in order to make it valid in the eyes of the law. And it must be signed in the presence of three witnesses who are *not* also beneficiaries of the will. (Some states require only two witnesses, but use three to be safe.)

Exercise

Follow these simple steps:

1) Sit down with a pad and pencil sometime while you're watching television (since none of us ever really gives our full attention to TV anyway) and make a list of all your worldly possessions. Put everything down: house, furniture, car, wardrobe, jewelry, tools, book collection, exercise bicycle, stereo system, record/cd collection, photo albums, the ugly macramé hanging your Aunt Clara made for you in the '70s that you take out only when she comes over for dinner ...everything.

Take your time putting this list together. Keep it on the night stand next to your bed, and take it to work with you. When you think of something, jot it down.

Don't forget your bank account(s), your brokerage account(s), your pension plan at work, your life insurance policy, or any other financial assets. And be sure to list all the debts you owe: mortgage, auto loans, student loan, credit cards, personal line(s) of credit, equity line(s) of credit, personal notes, or whatever.

2) Beside each entry, list the name of the person you would want to have that item. (It won't be necessary to do that with your debts.) Be creative, be devilish (leave your pet tarantula to Aunt Clara, for example), but be thorough. When you have completed your list, you have the beginnings of your will. The hard part is over.

3) Think of a couple of people you trust enough to carry out your directions. One person is your first

choice, the other is your second. List them as your chosen executors. (Again, your first choice will usually be your spouse, if you have one.)

4) Include a sentence about which state you live in, and mention that you are "of sound mind and body" and that no one is making you do this.

5) Type your list, take it to work, and have three of your fellow employees watch you sign it and date it. Have them sign it and date it.

Congratulations, you now have a will.

If you're married, you and your spouse could create a *joint will* where you leave everything to each other first, and then to either your children or other people if you should die at the same time.

What If I Need to Make Changes in My Will?

If you need to add or change something in your will, you simply write a *codicil* (taken from the Latin word *codicillus,* having to do with ancient books of laws). A codicil is a mini-version of your will. It must contain the same legal mumbo jumbo about your state of mind and your state of residence, and it must be signed by three witnesses (although you don't have to use the same three who signed your original will).

Adding something to your will (you just bought a tent trailer, for example) is a one-step process. You merely say in your codicil that you are adding the tent trailer to your list of assets, and you mention who you would like to leave it to.

Changing something in your will (you move to a new house, or you decide you want to leave your stereo to someone else) is a two-step process:

1) You must first *revoke* the portion of your original will you want to change: "I hereby revoke the portion of my will that states:" (and then quote the *exact* words from your will that you are changing).

2) Then you make your change: "Instead, I wish to make the following provision(s):" (and then list your new home address or the name of the person who will now get your stereo).

What Do I Do with My Will Once It Is Drawn Up?

Common sense tells you to put your completed will in your safety deposit box at the bank. But if you do, then you should also be sure the bank has a written notice from you on file that clearly says your spouse and/or your executor can have immediate access to the box upon your death. Otherwise, the bank will probably be required to seal the box (because it is one of your assets!) until the probate process begins.

Making copies of your will can also be a very tricky proposition. If you want to make copies, copy only *unsigned* versions.

Here is why: Only *signed* wills are legal. Let's say you want to make 20 copies of your will and send them to all the people you are leaving something to. Then in five years, you change your mind: you no longer want to leave your coffee mug to your next door neighbor. If you had already sent a *signed* copy of your will to that neighbor, he or she could show up in court when you die and legally demand that coffee mug. If you sent an *unsigned* copy of the will, he or she would have no case. So if you feel you must distribute copies of your will, send unsigned copies, and create only one signed version. It will make the probate process much easier. (See Appendix B.)

What Exactly Is Probate Anyway?

The word probate comes from the Latin word *probare*, meaning "to prove." Probate is simply the process of your executor and beneficiaries proving to the courts that your final wishes are being carried out. The easiest, quickest way to provide that proof is with your final written testament.

"So if you feel you must distribute copies of your will, send unsigned copies, and create only one signed version."

Probate is sometimes a time-consuming, expensive process, and sometimes it is not. It all depends on a number of variables, including the size of your estate, the probate judge's mood, how thorough your will is, how prepared your executor and/or attorney is, and the number of creditors your estate must satisfy before your property can be distributed, among others.

Can I Avoid Probate?

If an estate is small enough, chances are good your beneficiaries can avoid probate. If your assets are held jointly with your spouse, full ownership should automatically revert to him or her.

If your estate is large enough (usually above $600,000), and you want to avoid probate, you might consider a living trust.

What Is a Living Trust?

A living trust transfers title of your property to a trust while you are still living. You can transfer your home, your investment portfolio, jewelry, or any other tangible asset you hold title to. Once you have created the living trust, you technically do not own the property anymore; the trust does. But you continue to control the property.

The idea here is to avoid the probate process when you die. With a living trust, when you die, control of the trust legally transfers to your beneficiaries. Since title of the property itself is not transferred, there is nothing to probate.

"Once you have created the living trust, you technically do not own the property anymore; the trust does."

There are three parties involved in any trust:

- *The grantor*, or creator, of the trust. That's you.

- *The trustee(s)* of the trust, who oversee its administration. This is probably you and your spouse, or you and a trusted friend or relative. (It's always a good idea to have more than one trustee in case one of you becomes incapacitated.)

- *The beneficiaries* of the trust, usually your children or whomever you designate to take control of your property when you die.

There are two kinds of living trusts: *revocable* and *irrevocable*.

Revocable living trusts

This is a living trust that you can change over the years as conditions change.

Advantage: Revocable trusts are very flexible. For example, if you name your daughter and son-in-law as beneficiaries of the trust and they divorce, you can remove the son-in-law, if you want to.

Disadvantage: You create more paperwork for yourself; you must remember to keep everything *(everything)* in the name of the trust; and if you make your revocable trust the beneficiary of your 401(k) or other pension plans, you *cannot* roll those plans over the way you normally would.

Irrevocable living trusts

This is a living trust that you cannot change after it has been created.

Advantage: People normally create irrevocable trusts for tax purposes. Once you have transferred title of property to an irrevocable trust, you personally are no longer liable for the taxes on the income generated by that property. Either the trust is liable, or the beneficiaries of the property are liable.

Disadvantage: The main disadvantage of an irrevocable trust is that you cannot change it. You must be absolutely certain the trust is created *exactly* the way you want it.

"There is no way you can create a living trust by yourself. It must be done with the help of a qualified attorney."

There is *no way* you can create a living trust by yourself. It must be done with the help of a qualified attorney. He or she will have you fill out a standard form, creating your trust. And he or she should counsel you on whether you should create a revocable or an irrevocable trust.

Then you must change the title on all property you own. Instead of your home being legally owned by YOU and YOUR SPOUSE, it would now be owned by YOU and YOUR SPOUSE, TRUSTEES OF YOUR FAMILY TRUST, DATED (MONTH)(DAY)(YEAR). The same will go for your cars, bank accounts, brokerage accounts, your checking account...everything where you hold legal title.

Do I Still Need a Will If I Create a Living Trust?

Probably. You will still need a will:

- If you have children who are minors, your will identifies whom you want to act as legal custodian for them if you should die prematurely.

- If you have retirement accounts you may want to roll over periodically. You cannot roll them over if they are held in trust.

- To dispose of life insurance benefits.

- To dispose of property that is not held in joint tenancy.

Summary

You worked hard to accumulate the assets in your estate (even if your estate consists of only one coffee mug). So you should decide who gets those assets when you die. That is the purpose of a will and/or a living trust.

You should not be afraid to create a will and/or a trust. Yes, it takes some time to think about what you want in the will and/or the trust and to decide who gets what. But, no, it is not a very expensive proposition to create one, and finding a qualified attorney is not all that difficult.

The scope of this book does not really do the estate planning process justice. It is subject to a myriad of federal and state laws and regulations. The purpose of this chapter is merely to demystify the process. Yes, you can write a will and/or a living trust. And, indeed, you *must*.

When you are ready, consult with a qualified attorney or a comprehensive publication.

STEP 10

Start Your Children on the Road to Prosperity

The best ways to save for their college education

> **WARNING:** If You Are Thinking About Starting a Family, Reading This Chapter Could Materially Alter Those Plans.

There is bad news, and there is good news when it comes to saving for your child's college education. The bad news, of course, is the cost. The good news is there are a number of ways for you to successfully save for and/or finance those costs.

Let's go over the biggest issues facing anyone who is saving for college.

Issue #1: How Much Will a College Education Cost When My Child Is Ready to Attend?

A college education is expensive. And the odds are it will be a lot more expensive in 10–20 years. But the fact is that no one knows for sure exactly how much a college education will cost in a decade or two. So saving for your child's tuition and other college-related expenses is like aiming at a moving target.

The best *guesstimates* about future college costs come from the College Board, best known for producing the Scholastic Aptitude Test (SAT) college entrance exams. It tracks the increasing costs at both public and private colleges and universities.

Table 10-1 shows what four years at public and private colleges may cost between now and the year 2017. The projections are based on the College Board's annual estimate of costs for 1993–94, and they assume an annual cost increase of 7 percent, which is — on average — how much costs rose between 1982 and 1992.

Note: The column on the left represents the year your child starts college, and the next two columns show how much *all four years* of college might cost.

Example: Let's assume your child's freshman year of college begins in the fall of 2008. If he or she attends a public college, this chart says that you are likely to spend $88,309 over four years for tuition, books, fees, room and board, and other living expenses.

Note: The costs in the table *do not* include travel, fraternity/sorority expenses, and other additional costs you might incur. And it assumes that your child will be able to earn a degree in four years, which the vast majority of students today do not do.

Table 10-1

PROJECTED COLLEGE COSTS

Your Child's Freshman Year	Four Years at a Public College	Four Years at a Private College
1994	$34,248	$71,384
1995	$36,645	$76,381
1996	$39,210	$81,727
1997	$41,955	$87,448
1998	$44,892	$93,570
1999	$48,034	$100,120
2000	$51,397	$107,128
2001	$54,994	$114,627
2002	$58,844	$122,651
2003	$62,963	$131,236
2004	$67,371	$140,423
2005	$72,087	$150,252
2006	$77,133	$160,770
2007	$82,532	$172,024
2008	$88,309	$184,066
2009	$94,491	$196,950
2010	$101,105	$210,737
2011	$108,183	$225,489
2012	$115,755	$241,273
2013	$123,859	$258,162
2014	$132,529	$276,233
2015	$141,806	$295,570
2016	$151,732	$316,260
2017	$162,353	$338,398

source: *The College Board* 1993–94 Survey

There are a number of things that could keep costs from rising this much, including the following:

Inflation could remain low throughout the rest of the '90s and into the next decade. While this could slow future increases in tuition, you should be aware that, in the past, college costs have *not* been tied directly to the national inflation rate. Typically, they have risen faster.

Enrollment could begin to fall appreciably. This could happen either because the demand for a college education in the workplace of the future declines (in which case you would probably see a rise in enrollment at trade schools), or it could happen simply because fewer people will be able to afford high tuition costs.

The government could mandate a cap on education costs sometime in the future. Witness the efforts by the Clinton administration to do the same thing to health care costs.

Issue #2: How Much Will I Need to Save Each Month in Order to Meet the Projected Costs?

Figuring this out involves some simple math. Table 10-2 will help you figure out how much money you will need to put away each month in order to hit your projected cost target. Here is how it works:

1) From Table 10-1, choose the total four-year cost based on the year your child will enter his or her freshman year.

2) From Table 10-2, choose the "savings factor" from the right-hand column based on your child's current age, which is listed in the left-hand column.

3) Total four-year cost x Savings factor = The amount of money you will need to save each year in order to meet projected costs of a four-year college education.

Example: Let's use the same example we used for Table 10-1. We know that if your child first attends a public college in the fall of 2008, you can expect to pay roughly $88,309 over four years. If your child is currently four years old, Table 10-2 says your savings factor is 0.034. Multiply $88,309 by 0.034. The result is $3,002. That is how much money you need to save each year in order to meet your child's expected college-related expenses beginning in the fall of 2008.

"If your child first attends a public college in the fall of 2008, you can expect to pay roughly $88,309 over four years."

Table 10-2

Age of Child	Savings Factor
1	0.025
2	0.027
3	0.031
4	0.034
5	0.038
6	0.043
7	0.049
8	0.056
9	0.064
10	0.074
11	0.087
12	0.104
13	0.126
14	0.158
15	0.205
16	0.285
17	0.445
18	0.926

source: Founders Funds College Cost Worksheet. The savings factor assumes a hypothetical average return of 8 percent, which would represent a balanced investment mix of stocks and bonds, and it does *not* take into account any taxes paid.

A Few Alternatives to Consider

Before we go on, you should realize that the projections above are *targets* for you to aim for. If you don't think you can save that much, it does *not* mean your child will be unable to attend college. What it does mean is you should consider your alternatives.

"80 percent of those who qualified who attended a private for-profit college received some kind of federal financial aid."

1) Your child could attend a college near your home. That would save you the costs of room and board.

2) Your child could work before and/or during college to help pay expenses.

3) Your child could first attend a two-year community college in order to complete basic degree requirements at a lower cost.

4) Your child could earn a full or partial athletic or academic scholarship.

5) Your child could take out a student loan.

6) You could qualify for financial aid. A study conducted by the National Center for Education Statistics published in May of 1993, found that in 1990 (the year for which the most recent data were available) an astounding 71 percent of all undergraduates in America qualified for some form of federal financial aid, whether they received it or not.

- *80 percent* of those who qualified who attended a private for-profit college received some kind of federal financial aid.

- *49 percent* of those who qualified who attended a private not-for-profit college received some kind of federal financial aid.

- *29 percent* of those who qualified who attended a public college received some form of federal financial aid.

7) Your child could try to earn a bachelor's degree in three years, instead of the traditional four. Believe it or not, it could save you anywhere from 25–50 percent.

8) You could consider the Clinton administration's college service program, where your child helps pay for college by performing one or two years of community service.

9) Depending on your child's future career choice, he or she may want to consider a less expensive trade school.

10) For some young people, military service is still a terrific way to get a college education.

Later in the chapter, I will go over several financial aid programs available to help finance the cost of a college education. But first, if you plan to save the money yourself, let's go over some simple rules of thumb of how to invest it.

Issue #3: How Do I Invest the Money I'm Saving for College?

Here are a couple of things to keep in mind:

1) The first rule of saving for your child's college education is to start early. Ideally, that means starting when your child is born.

2) Second, try to save a constant amount. Either use Table 10-2 to determine how much you need to save each year in order to meet the expected cost of sending your child to college, or else determine on your own how much you will realistically be able to set aside each month.

Here is the strategy you should use to determine how and where to invest the money you are saving for college. Divide your child's years before college into three periods: Birth–10, 10–15, and 15–22.

Birth–10 years old: 100% Aggressive Growth

"You should be trying to earn 'double digit returns' while your child is still in 'single digits.'"

These are the years when you need to be the most aggressive with your investment strategy. I like to say that you should be trying to earn "double digit returns" while your child is still in "single digits." You can afford to take greater investment risks now because you still have plenty of time before you will need the money. Taking risks now could provide you with a greater rate of return than you would get from more conservative savings and investment vehicles such as passbook savings accounts, money market funds, or certificates of deposit.

These are typically the years when you should look to invest in stocks that have the greatest growth potential. You'll have to do some homework to determine which ones those are, but generally speaking:

- Look for companies developing products and services that will eventually improve the quality of our lives and make them more efficient.

- Think about investing in other countries where the national growth rate may be greater than here in the United States for the next decade or so.

If you don't have time for all the homework, there are *plenty* of mutual funds to choose from. A mutual fund pools your money with other investors and invests in stocks and/or bonds, depending on the type of mutual fund. When your child is very young, you should be looking for mutual funds with a *growth* or *aggressive growth* investment objective. (See Chapter 4 for a more thorough discussion of mutual funds.)

Note: If you consider yourself conservative, and you are uneasy about committing all your money to more volatile investments at this point, consider devoting some of your money to zero coupon bonds. These are bonds that do not pay any interest until they mature. Instead, they continue to grow faster than a normal bond because of the accumulating compound interest. Choose a zero coupon bond, or a zero coupon bond fund, that will mature a year or two before your child enters college.

"It's okay to accept 'single digit returns' when your child hits 'double digits.'"

10–15 years old:
50% Aggressive Growth/Growth
50% Income

During these years, you might not want to be quite as aggressive. That is, it's okay to accept "single digit returns" when your child hits "double digits." Think about devoting half the money you're saving to growth stocks, and invest the other half in bonds or more conservative blue chip stocks that pay a dividend. If you choose to invest your money through mutual funds, look for funds in the *growth & income* or *income–equity* or *income-bond* categories. And be sure to automatically re-invest the dividends you earn.

Note for conservative investors: Think about United States savings bonds during these years. They pay a higher return than money market funds or certificates of deposit, and if you buy them during these years they will mature just before your child is ready to attend college. And if you buy them specifically to help pay for college, the interest earned is tax-free.

15–22 years old:
80% Capital Preservation
20% Income

These are the years to be conservative with your investments for college. By now, you should be completely out of your aggressive growth investments, and you should begin moving your old money into accounts that preserve your principal.

Think about investing in certificates of deposit that will mature as your child is entering college. Then, when your child enters college you should have a portion of your money in either an interest-bearing checking account or a money market fund with check-writing privileges. That way, you can pay college bills and earn some interest at the same time.

In order to keep up with the rate of inflation, continue to invest new money in income-bearing funds and accounts.

A number of mutual fund companies have developed college savings programs that are quite good. With some of them, you can arrange to have a predetermined amount of money automatically withdrawn from your savings or checking account each month. The money is then systematically invested in mutual funds best suited to your needs.

At least one mutual fund company, Twentieth Century Mutual Funds, has a program where — depending on how old your child is when you start investing — the money you invest is automatically transferred from aggressive growth funds to more conservative income funds as your child gets older. And by the time your child reaches college age, all your money is in a money market fund with check-writing privileges.

Note: At the end of this chapter, I list a number of mutual fund companies with specially designed college savings programs.

Do I put the college savings accounts in my name or in my child's name?

If you decide to put college savings accounts in your child's name, they will undoubtedly be custodial accounts known as either *UTMA* or *UGMA* accounts.

—UTMA stands for Uniform Transfer to Minors Act.

—UGMA stands for Uniform Gifts to Minors Act.

The difference is an UTMA account allows you to give your child any kind of property, and that property can be bequeathed to the account through a will. UGMA account rules are more restrictive. They allow only bank deposits, securities (including mutual funds), and insurance policies to be held in an UGMA. And you may not bequeath any property to an UGMA.

If you decide to open an account in your child's name, the type of account you open depends on the state you live in. Some states are UTMA states, and some are UGMA states.

UGMA States & Territories

Canal Zone	Mississippi	Tennessee
Connecticut	Nebraska	Texas
Delaware	New York	Vermont
Guam	Pennsylvania	Virgin Islands
Michigan	South Carolina	

UTMA States & Territories

Alabama	Kansas	North Carolina
Alaska	Kentucky	North Dakota
Arkansas	Louisiana	Ohio
California	Maine	Oklahoma
Colorado	Maryland	Oregon
Dist. of Columbia	Massachusetts	Rhode Island
Florida	Minnesota	South Dakota
Georgia	Missouri	Utah
Hawaii	Montana	Virginia
Idaho	Nevada	Washington
Illinois	New Hampshire	West Virginia
Indiana	New Jersey	Wisconsin
Iowa	New Mexico	Wyoming

Note: Arizona allows either account to be opened.

An UTMA or UGMA account will be in your child's name, and you will be listed as the custodian. When your child reaches age 18 or 21, depending on the state you live in, he or she will take control of the account.

Advantage:

The main advantage of creating an UTMA or UGMA custodial account for your child has to do with taxes. If the account is in your name, you will pay taxes on any interest, dividends, or capital gains earned.

If the account is in your child's name, with you listed as the custodian, the IRS says a child under age 14 does not pay taxes on the first $600 the account earns. The next $600 is taxed at the child's tax rate (presumably lower than yours), and any earnings over $1,200 are taxed at your rate.

Once your child reaches age 14, all income will be taxed at his or her rate, which — again — will presumably be lower than your tax rate.

Disadvantages:

1) I've heard people argue that a custodial account is a bad idea because even though you may have set it up for future college expenses, once the child reaches the so-called age of majority, she or he can legally decide *not* to spend the money on college.

It is certainly a valid point to keep in mind, but here is a warning to my own children: *Don't get any big ideas.*

2) There is a more serious matter to consider: A college savings account in your child's name may hamper his or her ability to qualify for financial aid.

Most financial aid packages require your child to contribute as much as 35 percent of the assets in his or her name to annual college costs, while parents are liable for only 5.6 percent of their savings.

So there is the possibility that the amount you save in your child's name — while it may not turn out to be enough to meet all your child's college expenses — could be too much to qualify for additional financial aid.

Important Note: Financial aid programs do *not* consider money you have in tax-deferred programs like 401(k)s or 403(b)s when calculating what a parent must contribute to a child's college expenses.

Issue #4: What If I Need Help? What Kind of Financial Aid Is Available?

This is the best news of all. There are quite a number of financial aid programs available.

There are generally three kinds:

- Scholarships, grants, and fellowships.
- Loans.
- Work study programs.

Scholarships, Grants, and Fellowships

This is money you don't have to repay. It is awarded for academic or athletic achievement, demonstrated talent (musical or otherwise), or a child's ability to perform some type of service.

Local civic, fraternal, and professional organizations are usually the best sources. There are also a number of philanthropic trusts and foundations around the country that target students with specific needs.

And, of course, most colleges and universities are in a position to offer partial or full scholarships to qualified students.

The United States Department of Education has two college grant programs:

Federal Pell Grants: This is the largest federal grant program in the country. It provides undergraduate students with grants of between $400 and $2,300, depending on a student's needs.

FSEOG: These are Federal Supplemental Educational Opportunity Grants. They provide grants as high as $4,000 to students with a greater need than those who qualify for Federal Pell Grants.

The best place to start your search for scholarships and grants is either your child's high school guidance counselor's office or your local university's financial aid office.

Important Note: Be wary of private companies that provide scholarship "tip sheets" for a price, or of companies that claim they can match you with available scholarship funds. Be especially wary if they use the word "guarantee." Check with your local Better Business Bureau before you ever do business with such a company.

Loans

This is money that must be repaid. The size of the loan and the repayment schedule are often determined by your financial need.

The United States Department of Education is the largest source of college loans. Some of the more prominent loan programs include the following.

Federal Perkins Loans: These are low interest fixed-rate loans where qualified undergraduate students may borrow up to $3,000 for each year of study, up to a maximum of $15,000. Graduate students can borrow up to $5,000 each academic year, up to a maximum $30,000 on the total loan (and that includes what you may have borrowed as an undergraduate).

You must be a full-time student to qualify for a Federal Perkins Loan. And you must begin paying the loan back after you graduate, if you leave school, or if you stop taking a full academic load. The government usually allows ten years to repay the loan.

Federal Stafford Loans: These are variable-rate loans where — regardless of need — students may borrow up to $23,000 over the course˙ of their undergraduate study. Graduate students and students in professional programs may borrow up to $65,000.

Students must pay an origination fee to secure these loans: 5 percent for federally subsidized loans and 6.5 percent for unsubsidized loans.

Federal Stafford Loans are usually arranged through private lenders like banks, credit unions, or savings and loans. And like Federal Perkins Loan recipients, students must maintain a full academic schedule to qualify for Federal Stafford Loans.

Students normally have ten years to repay the loan.

Federal Supplemental Loans for Students (SLS): This loan program is similar to the Stafford program. The main difference is it allows students to attend school part–time.

Federal PLUS Loans: PLUS stands for Parent Loans for Undergraduate Students. These are variable-rate loans for parents with children who attend college either full– or part–time.

The size of the loan is determined by the child's college costs minus any financial aid already received.

State governments also have loan programs for undergraduate and graduate students. Check with your state's department of education for information.

Note: At the end of this chapter, I provide an address where you can get more information about college loan programs.

Work Study

These are programs where students work at part- or full-time jobs either on or off campus, and part or all of the wages earned are used to supplement college expenses.

The *Federal Work-Study Program* is a prime example. It tries to place students in jobs that are related to their area of study. And a student's work schedule is coordinated with her or his school schedule each semester. The time to ask about work-study programs is when you apply to a particular college or university.

Note: The Better Business Bureau has a terrific brochure called *Tips On Financial Aid for College.* Call your local BBB office for a free copy.

Summary

Saving for your child's college education is obviously a daunting task. But it becomes easier if you first determine:

1) How much it may cost you.

2) How much you are capable of saving.

3) The best places to invest the money you are saving for college.

4) What your financing alternatives are.

Who to Call

For more information about student loan programs, write or call for the brochure offered by the United Student Aid (USA) Funds.

> P.O. Box 6180
> Indianapolis, IN 46206–6180
> (800) LOAN–USA

The College Board, which is a nonprofit association that helps people find financing for college, also publishes the annual *College Costs and Financial Aid Handbook*, available in most bookstores. It also has a database of national, state, public, and private scholarship information called the *College Cost Explorer FUND FINDER*, and a software package called ExPAN that helps you find ways to pay for college.

> *The College Board*
> Guidance Publishing
> 45 Columbus Ave.
> New York, NY 10023–6992
> (212) 713–8000

Here is a list of five mutual fund companies that offer college savings programs.

> *Founders Funds*
> Founders Financial Center
> 2930 East Third Ave.
> Denver, CO 80206
> (303) 394–4404
> (800) 525–2440

Ask for the *Founders Guide to Planning for College Education.*

> *Franklin/Templeton Group*
> 777 Mariners Island Blvd.
> P.O. Box 777
> San Mateo, CA 94403–9877
> (800) 342–5236

Ask for the *Franklin College Costs Planner.*

Neuberger & Berman
605 Third Ave.
New York, NY 10158–0006
(212) 476–8800
(800) 877–9700

Ask for their *College Planning Kit* (including a terrific brochure called *12 Tips for College Savers*).

Twentieth Century Mutual Funds
P.O. Box 419200
Kansas City, MO 64141–6200
(816) 531–5575
(800) 345–2021

Ask about their excellent *College Investment Program.*

T. Rowe Price
100 East Pratt St.
Baltimore, MD 21202
(800) 638–5660
In Baltimore: 547–2308

Ask for their *College Planning Kit.*

ONE MORE STEP

Enjoy Your Journey to Prosperity
A ten-part checklist

Achieving financial prosperity today is a more complicated challenge than it was a generation or two ago. We have more tax laws to keep up with, more retirement plans and insurance products to choose from, more savings and investment vehicles to learn about, more estate planning procedures to pursue. It's enough to make any grown-up want to stay in bed in the fetal position all day.

However, I am fully convinced that we all can, and indeed *must*, get it done. How? One step at a time.

It would be impossible to accomplish all I have outlined in this book overnight.

Suggestion: Take a whole year to develop and implement your plan.

But, above all, enjoy your journey to prosperity.

Here is a checklist to help you put together your plan of attack:

1) Do You Have Any Financial Goals?

- How much money do you need to save for retirement?

- How much money do you need to save for your child's college education?

2) Are You Budget-ized?

- Do you have a monthly budget that assigns a role to each dollar you earn?

- Are you reducing the number of Deficit Dollars and increasing the number of Prosperity Dollars in your budget?

- In order to meet your short-term financial goals, and any emergencies or opportunities that come up, have you built, or are you building, a reserve account of money that represents at least three (and ideally six) months worth of your expenses?

3) Do You Have a Lifetime Investment Plan?

- Do you understand the risks involved with investing?

- Are you a saver, an investor, or a speculator?

- Do you have a systematic investment plan designed to meet your long-term financial goals?

4) Are You Using Mutual Funds to Help Achieve Financial Prosperity?

- Do you understand the risks involved with investing through mutual funds?

- Are you aware of the many kinds of mutual funds available, and which ones can best meet your investment objectives?

5) Do You Have a Do-It-Yourself Retirement Plan?

- Are you saving enough money for retirement?

- Are you contributing the maximum amount of money allowed to an employer-sponsored 401(k) or 403(b) retirement? Or are you contributing the maximum allowed to a personal Individual Retirement Account or Keogh Plan?

- Do you know how much money Social Security will pay you each month when you retire?

6) Is Your Home a Nest Egg or Just a Nest?

- If you're planning to buy a house, have you developed an effective way to save for the down payment and closing costs?

- Have you chosen a mortgage that will help you build equity in your home as quickly as possible?

- Should you refinance your current mortgage in order to cut down on interest costs?

- Do you need more retirement income now? What about a reverse mortgage?

7) Are You Properly Managing Your Level of Debt?

- Do you have too many Deficit Dollars in your monthly budget?

- Have you developed a systematic plan of reducing those Deficit Dollars?

8) Do You Have Enough Insurance?

- Do you have the right kind of life insurance policy to meet your personal needs?

- Do you have enough disability insurance to help you pay your bills if you can't work for up to a year or even longer?

• Do you have enough health insurance coverage? Is it the right kind to meet your family's needs? Are you paying too much for it?

9) What About Your Estate Plan?

• Have you drawn up a will?

• Have you thought about a living trust?

10) Have You Started Your Children on the Road to Prosperity?

• Are you putting money away each month for your child's college education?

• Will it be enough to meet all your child's expected college-related expenses?

• If not, how will you pay the rest of the expenses? Loans? Scholarships? Work-study programs?

Appendix A

Budget Modules

1. Your budget worksheet

2. Your monthly budget

3. Your retirement nest egg

4. Your child's college fund

5. Sample reports

Getting Started by Installing the *Budget Modules* on Your Computer

Bill Griffeth's Ten Steps to Financial Prosperity *Budget Modules* contain simple-to-use worksheet templates compatible with popular software packages such as Lotus, Quattro or Excel. To get started working on your own budget and savings plan, simply "RETRIEVE" the appropriate version of the BUDGET files based on the spreadsheet software that you use. For spreadsheet software not mentioned, the Lotus version is most compatible for importing into other programs. (As with any software, for your protection we recommend that you make a backup copy of the original diskette.)

Software Requirements	File Name
Lotus 123 version 2.2 or higher	BUDGET1.WK1
Quattro version 1.0 or higher	BUDGET2.WQ1
Excel version 4.0 or higher	BUDGET3.XLS

In retrieving the file, the first screen to appear will be the MAIN MENU, as shown on page 216. You can begin working in any module by either using the "GO TO" function, in most spreadsheet software that is the "F5" key, or by simply moving your cursor to the "address" shown on the main menu, for example the address of YOUR BUDGET WORKSHEET is cell A1. Once you are working in the modules you should simply use the functions that you are familiar with as a spreadsheet user. To move from one module to another, simply use your "GO TO" function or return to the MAIN MENU to make a selection.

Don't worry about wrecking the modules! Only the data input cells are unprotected. If you try to make a change to a cell that contains a formula or label you will be reminded that the protection prevents you from making that entry. However, if you are an experienced spreadsheet user, and you wish to make changes to the basic functions of the worksheets, simply unprotect cells you wish to modify and make your own changes.

Now that you are ready to get to work, simply follow the step-by-step guidelines found in this Appendix A. If you get stuck, turn to page 233, where you will find a complete set of sample reports with data filled in for you — these examples show you exactly how your own reports should appear once you have filled in all of your own financial data. Good luck on your road to financial prosperity!

MAIN MENU	
"Command"	
Go To (F5) A1	1) **YOUR BUDGET WORKSHEET:** Steps to setting up a workable monthly budget
Go To (F5) A58	2) **YOUR MONTHLY BUDGET:** Keep track of your monthly expenses
Go To (F5) A172	3) **YOUR RETIREMENT NEST EGG:** Determine how much money you need to save each month to meet your retirement goals
Go To (F5) A225	4) **YOUR CHILD'S COLLEGE FUND:** Determine how much money you need to save each month to meet your child's college expenses

1. Your Budget Worksheet

Your Budget Worksheet has two purposes:

1) To help you determine where your money goes each month.

2) To help you develop a workable monthly budget.

Step 1: The worksheet is divided into three categories:

1) *Prosperity Dollars:* These are the dollars you use to save for short term financial goals, emergencies and obligations like vacations and insurance premiums. These are also the dollars you invest to meet long term financial goals like retirement and your child's college education.

2) *Budget Dollars:* These are the dollars you use to pay your monthly bills, including your mortgage.

3) *Deficit Dollars:* These are the dollars you use to pay-off your installment debts: your credit cards, your auto loans, any lines of credit you may have, or any personal notes.

Determine whether your monthly budget contains any items other than those listed in the ITEM column. If so, simply type over the items listed as "Other" with your own budget items.

Step 2: Go back through your checkbook and credit card statements to determine the amounts you spent for each of your expense items over the past three months. Or, over the next three months, fill in the actual amounts that you spend on each item. Be sure to include any items that may occur only annually or semi-annually. See Exhibit 1.

Enter these amounts in the appropriate monthly columns.

Note: For each expense item you use, it is necessary to enter an amount for each month, even if the amount entered is zero. If you leave any blanks, an error message will appear, requiring you to go back and make sure you have completed entries for all three months. (You do not, however, need to use *all* of the expense categories listed in the ITEM column, only use as many as you need for your own circumstances.)

Step 3: As each amount is entered, the AVERAGE column will automatically compute the average amount spent per month to date. At the end of three months, evaluate each amount displayed in the AVERAGE column. Are you spending too much for that item? Could you spend less? If so, where would you devote the extra money each month: Your retirement account? Your college account? Where? Fill in the TARGET column with the amounts you feel you can comfortably devote to each budget item each month. That amount will automatically be displayed in the BUDGET column of *Your Monthly Budget.*

Step 4: (Optional) To print *Your Budget Worksheet,* follow your own program's print instructions. The print range can be identified as "budgetworksheet" or A1..F56.

Exhibit 1

Shaded boxes highlight user data entry fields.

YOUR BUDGET WORKSHEET					
ITEM	MONTH 1	MONTH 2	MONTH 3	AVERAGE	TARGET
PROSPERITY DOLLARS					
Reserve Account				$0.00	
Retirement Account				$0.00	
College Fund				$0.00	
TOTAL PROSPERITY DOLLARS	$0.00	$0.00	$0.00	$0.00	$0.00
BUDGET DOLLARS					
Mortgage/Rent				$0.00	
Telephone				$0.00	
Electricity				$0.00	
Water/Sewer				$0.00	
Gas/Heating Oil				$0.00	
Insurance				$0.00	
Groceries				$0.00	
Miscellaneous				$0.00	
Other				$0.00	
Other				$0.00	
Other				$0.00	
Other				$0.00	
Other				$0.00	
TOTAL BUDGET DOLLARS	$0.00	$0.00	$0.00	$0.00	$0.00
DEFICIT DOLLARS					
Credit Card #1				$0.00	
Credit Card #2				$0.00	
Auto Loan #1				$0.00	
Auto Loan #2				$0.00	
Other				$0.00	
Other				$0.00	
Other				$0.00	
TOTAL DEFICIT DOLLARS	$0.00	$0.00	$0.00	$0.00	$0.00
TOTAL DOLLARS SPENT	$0.00	$0.00	$0.00	$0.00	$0.00

2. Your Monthly Budget

The purpose of *Your Monthly Budget* is to provide you with an easy-to-use spreadsheet that automatically shows you where you are spending your money. It will also show you where you are over and under budget.

Here is how to use it:

Step 1: Fill in the beginning month and year as a *label* (e.g. 'January 1995) in the title of the worksheet. See Exhibit 2. Note, that an error message will appear if you do not enter the date in this format. If you completed *Your Budget Worksheet*, skip to Step 3.

The worksheet is divided into three categories:

1) *Prosperity Dollars:* These are the dollars you use to save for short term financial goals, emergencies and obligations like vacations and insurance premiums. These are also the dollars you invest to meet long term financial goals like retirement and your child's college education.

2) *Budget Dollars:* These are the dollars you use to pay your monthly bills, including your mortgage.

3) *Deficit Dollars:* These are the dollars you use to pay-off your installment debts: your credit cards, your auto loans, any lines of credit you may have, or any personal notes.

Determine whether your monthly budget contains any items other than those listed in the ITEM column. If so, simply type over the items listed as "Other" with your own budget items.

Note: It is not necessary to use every expense category listed in the ITEM column.

Step 2: Fill in the amount for each item in the BUDGET column that you feel accurately reflects the monthly cost of that item.

Step 3: Over the next twelve months, fill in the actual amounts that you spend on each item. See Exhibit 2.

Step 4: When you have completed a full month of entries, you can evaluate how well you have met *Your Monthly Budget*. Is there a budget deficit? Are you spending too much for certain items? Is there a budget surplus? If so, consider devoting it to either your RETIREMENT account, or your COLLEGE fund.

Step 5: (Optional) To print *Your Monthly Budget*, follow your own program's print instructions. The print range can be identified as "monthly_budget" or A57..H168.

Exhibit 2

Shaded boxes highlight user data entry fields.

YOUR MONTHLY BUDGET FOR YEAR BEGINNING

(Month Year)

ITEM	BUDGET	MONTH 1	MONTH 2	MONTH 3	MONTH 4	MONTH 5	MONTH 6
PROSPERITY DOLLARS							
Reserve Account	$0.00						
Retirement Account	$0.00						
College Fund	$0.00						
TOTAL PROSPERITY DOLLARS	$0.00	$0.00	$0.00	$0.00	$0.00	$0.00	$0.00
BUDGET DOLLARS							
Mortgage/Rent	$0.00						
Telephone	$0.00						
Electricity	$0.00						
Water/Sewer	$0.00						
Gas/Heating Oil	$0.00						
Insurance	$0.00						
Groceries	$0.00						
Miscellaneous	$0.00						
Other	$0.00						
Other	$0.00						
Other	$0.00						
Other	$0.00						
Other	$0.00						
TOTAL BUDGET DOLLARS	$0.00	$0.00	$0.00	$0.00	$0.00	$0.00	$0.00
DEFICIT DOLLARS							
Credit Card #1	$0.00						
Credit Card #2	$0.00						
Auto Loan #1	$0.00						
Auto Loan #2	$0.00						
Other	$0.00						
Other	$0.00						
Other	$0.00						
TOTAL DEFICIT DOLLARS	$0.00	$0.00	$0.00	$0.00	$0.00	$0.00	$0.00
TOTAL DOLLARS SPENT	$0.00	$0.00	$0.00	$0.00	$0.00	$0.00	$0.00
BUDGET SURPLUS/(DEFICIT)	$0.00	$0.00	$0.00	$0.00	$0.00	$0.00	$0.00

YOUR MONTHLY BUDGET FOR YEAR BEGINNING

ITEM	BUDGET	MONTH 7	MONTH 8	MONTH 9	MONTH 10	MONTH 11	MONTH 12
PROSPERITY DOLLARS							
Reserve Account	$0.00						
Retirement Account	$0.00						
College Fund	$0.00						
TOTAL PROSPERITY DOLLARS	$0.00	$0.00	$0.00	$0.00	$0.00	$0.00	$0.00
BUDGET DOLLARS							
Mortgage/Rent	$0.00						
Telephone	$0.00						
Electricity	$0.00						
Water/Sewer	$0.00						
Gas/Heating Oil	$0.00						
Insurance	$0.00						
Groceries	$0.00						
Miscellaneous	$0.00						
Other	$0.00						
Other	$0.00						
Other	$0.00						
Other	$0.00						
Other	$0.00						
TOTAL BUDGET DOLLARS	$0.00	$0.00	$0.00	$0.00	$0.00	$0.00	$0.00
DEFICIT DOLLARS							
Credit Card #1	$0.00						
Credit Card #2	$0.00						
Auto Loan #1	$0.00						
Auto Loan #2	$0.00						
Other	$0.00						
Other	$0.00						
Other	$0.00						
TOTAL DEFICIT DOLLARS	$0.00	$0.00	$0.00	$0.00	$0.00	$0.00	$0.00
TOTAL DOLLARS SPENT	$0.00	$0.00	$0.00	$0.00	$0.00	$0.00	$0.00
BUDGET SURPLUS/(DEFICIT)	$0.00	$0.00	$0.00	$0.00	$0.00	$0.00	$0.00

3. Your Retirement Nest Egg

The purpose of *Your Retirement Nest Egg* is to help you determine the total amount of money you will need to save for your retirement, and an amount you will need to save each month between now and retirement in order to achieve your goal. It is assumed that your annual investment earnings rate is conservatively set at 7 percent.

(If you prefer to use some other rate, simply type over the 7 percent with your own rate. Be realistic with your expectation.)

Refer to Exhibit 3 as you complete Steps 1-4.

Step 1: Enter the number of years remaining before you plan to retire. The number entered must be a whole number.

Step 2: Enter the amount of money you have currently saved for retirement.

Step 3: Enter the amount of money you feel you can comfortably devote to retirement savings each month.

Step 4: *Your Retirement Nest Egg* will produce two columns of numbers for you. The MONTHLY CONTRIBUTION column shows the monthly savings amount you selected in Step 3 and additional increments of $50. The RETIREMENT NEST EGG column represents the accumulated nest egg at retirement given the corresponding monthly savings amount and investment earnings rate.

Step 5: Refer to Exhibit 4. Select from the ANNUAL TARGET RETIREMENT INCOME column the amount that is approximately 70 percent of your current earnings. Next, select the MARKET INTEREST RATE you estimate will be in effect when you retire. (For example, in 1993, a conservatively invested nest egg returned about 5 percent.) Now move down the MARKET INTEREST RATE column you choose and match the TARGET RETIREMENT NEST EGG with the ANNUAL INCOME you chose. For example: If 70% of your current income is $30,000, and you feel you can earn 6% during your retirement years, your Target Nest Egg would be $500,000

Note: You should not have to withdraw any principal from this targeted nest egg in order to achieve the monthly income figure you chose in Exhibit 4. That income figure is interest-only, earned on your Retirement Nest Egg.

Step 6: Compare the nest egg amounts in Steps 4 and 5. Select from the MONTHLY CONTRIBUTION column on your screen, the amount which achieves your Targeted Retirement Nest Egg. Enter that amount in the TARGET column of *Your Budget Worksheet* or in the BUDGET column in *Your Monthly Budget.*

Note: If you don't feel you can afford to save this much money each month, here are a few suggestions:

1) Just do the best you can, saving as much as you can in a disciplined manner.

2) Consider being a bit more aggressive with your investments for retirement. Statistics show that more aggressive investments provide a greater return over long periods of time than conservative investments do. (See Table 3-1 on page 36.)

3) Realize that your nest egg may not be your only source of retirement income.

A) Social Security may still be able to supplement your income.

B) Your company pension (if you have one), or an employer-sponsored retirement benefit plan may also provide you with retirement income.

C) If you own a home, you might consider a reverse mortgage. (See page 148.)

Step 7: (Optional) To print *Your Retirement Nest Egg*, follow your own program's print instructions. The print range can be identified as "retirement_egg" or A169..F224.

Exhibit 3
Shaded boxes highlight user data entry fields.

YOUR RETIREMENT NEST EGG

Number of Years Remaining Before Retirement

Amount of Money Currently Saved for Retirement

Annual Investment Earnings Rate   7%

Monthly Savings for Retirement Account

Monthly Contribution	Retirement Nest Egg
$0	$0

Exhibit 4

Target Retirement Income		Target Retirement Nest Egg									
		Market Interest Rate									
Annual	Monthly	2%	4%	6%	8%	10%	12%	14%	16%	18%	20%
$18,000	$1,500	$900,000	$450,000	$300,000	$225,000	$180,000	$150,000	$128,571	$112,500	$100,000	$90,000
$24,000	$2,000	$1,200,000	$600,000	$400,000	$300,000	$240,000	$200,000	$171,429	$150,000	$133,333	$120,000
$30,000	$2,500	$1,500,000	$750,000	$500,000	$375,000	$300,000	$250,000	$214,286	$187,500	$166,667	$150,000
$36,000	$3,000	$1,800,000	$900,000	$600,000	$450,000	$360,000	$300,000	$257,143	$225,000	$200,000	$180,000
$42,000	$3,500	$2,100,000	$1,050,000	$700,000	$525,000	$420,000	$350,000	$300,000	$262,500	$233,333	$210,000
$48,000	$4,000	$2,400,000	$1,200,000	$800,000	$600,000	$480,000	$400,000	$342,857	$300,000	$266,667	$240,000
$54,000	$4,500	$2,700,000	$1,350,000	$900,000	$675,000	$540,000	$450,000	$385,714	$337,500	$300,000	$270,000
$60,000	$5,000	$3,000,000	$1,500,000	$1,000,000	$750,000	$600,000	$500,000	$428,571	$375,000	$333,333	$300,000
$66,000	$5,500	$3,300,000	$1,650,000	$1,100,000	$825,000	$660,000	$550,000	$471,429	$412,500	$366,667	$330,000
$72,000	$6,000	$3,600,000	$1,800,000	$1,200,000	$900,000	$720,000	$600,000	$514,286	$450,000	$400,000	$360,000
$78,000	$6,500	$3,900,000	$1,950,000	$1,300,000	$975,000	$780,000	$650,000	$557,143	$487,500	$433,333	$390,000
$84,000	$7,000	$4,200,000	$2,100,000	$1,400,000	$1,050,000	$840,000	$700,000	$600,000	$525,000	$466,667	$420,000
$90,000	$7,500	$4,500,000	$2,250,000	$1,500,000	$1,125,000	$900,000	$750,000	$642,857	$562,500	$500,000	$450,000
$96,000	$8,000	$4,800,000	$2,400,000	$1,600,000	$1,200,000	$960,000	$800,000	$685,714	$600,000	$533,333	$480,000
$102,000	$8,500	$5,100,000	$2,550,000	$1,700,000	$1,275,000	$1,020,000	$850,000	$728,571	$637,500	$566,667	$510,000
$108,000	$9,000	$5,400,000	$2,700,000	$1,800,000	$1,350,000	$1,080,000	$900,000	$771,429	$675,000	$600,000	$540,000
$114,000	$9,500	$5,700,000	$2,850,000	$1,900,000	$1,425,000	$1,140,000	$950,000	$814,286	$712,500	$633,333	$570,000
$200,000	$10,000	$6,000,000	$3,000,000	$2,000,000	$1,500,000	$1,200,000	$1,000,000	$857,143	$750,000	$666,667	$600,000

source: *The Delaware Group of Mutual Funds*

4. Your Child's College Fund

Your Child's College Fund is designed to help you determine how much money you will need to save each month in order to meet your child's/children's expected college expenses. It is assumed that your annual investment earnings rate is conservatively set at 7 percent.

(If you prefer to use some other rate, simply type over the 7 percent with your own rate. Be realistic with your expectation.)

Refer to Exhibit 5 as you complete Steps 1-3.

Step 1: Enter the number of years remaining before your child enters college. The number entered must be a whole number.

Step 2: Enter the amount of money you have currently saved for your child's college education.

Step 3: Enter the amount of money you feel you can comfortably devote to your child's college fund each month.

Step 4: *Your Child's College Fund* will produce two columns of numbers for you. The MONTHLY CONTRIBUTION column shows the monthly savings amount you selected in Step 3 and additional increments of $50. The CHILD'S COLLEGE FUND column represents the accumulated savings in the year your child enters college given the corresponding monthly savings amount and investment earnings rate.

Step 5: Refer to Exhibit 6. Select the year your child will enter college and the corresponding public or private college projected cost. Compare this cost with the CHILD'S COLLEGE FUND column on your screen.

Select from the MONTHLY CONTRIBUTION column the amount which reflects your desired college fund amount. Enter that amount in the TARGET column of *Your Budget Worksheet* or in the BUDGET column in *Your Monthly Budget.*

Step 6: If you have more than one child, simply repeat Steps 1-5, making a notation of the required monthly contribution for each child. Enter the total for all children into the TARGET column of *Your Budget Worksheet* or in the BUDGET column in *Your Monthly Budget.*

Note: If you don't feel you can afford to save that much money for your child's college education, there are a number of financing alternatives to consider. (See page 194.)

Step 7: (Optional) To print *Your Child's College Fund,* follow your own program's print instructions. The print range can be identified as "college_fund" or A225..E280.

Exhibit 5
Shaded boxes highlight user data entry fields.

YOUR CHILD'S COLLEGE FUND

Number of Years Until Child Enters College

Amount of Money Currently Saved for College

Annual Investment Earnings Rate   7%

Monthly Savings for College Fund

Monthly Contribution   Child's College Fund

$0 $0

Exhibit 6

PROJECTED COLLEGE COSTS

Your Child's Freshman Year	Four Years at a Public College	Four Years at a Private College
1994	$34,248	$71,384
1995	$36,645	$76,381
1996	$39,210	$81,727
1997	$41,955	$87,448
1998	$44,892	$93,570
1999	$48,034	$100,120
2000	$51,397	$107,128
2001	$54,994	$114,627
2002	$58,844	$122,651
2003	$62,963	$131,236
2004	$67,371	$140,423
2005	$72,087	$150,252
2006	$77,133	$160,770
2007	$82,532	$172,024
2008	$88,309	$184,066
2009	$94,491	$196,950
2010	$101,105	$210,737
2011	$108,183	$225,489
2012	$115,755	$241,273
2013	$123,859	$258,162
2014	$132,529	$276,233
2015	$141,806	$295,570
2016	$151,732	$316,260
2017	$162,353	$338,398

source: *The College Board* 1993–94 Survey

5. Sample Reports

YOUR BUDGET WORKSHEET

ITEM	MONTH 1	MONTH 2	MONTH 3	AVERAGE	TARGET
PROSPERITY DOLLARS					
Reserve Account	$250.00	$250.00	$250.00	$250.00	$250.00
Retirement Account	$0.00	$0.00	$0.00	$0.00	$400.00
College Fund	$0.00	$0.00	$0.00	$0.00	$129.00
TOTAL PROSPERITY DOLLARS	$250.00	$250.00	$250.00	$250.00	$779.00
BUDGET DOLLARS					
Mortgage/Rent	$1,047.00	$1,047.00	$1,047.00	$1,047.00	$1,047.00
Telephone	$52.00	$38.00	$47.00	$45.67	$45.00
Electricity	$63.00	$69.00	$65.00	$65.67	$65.00
Water/Sewer	$21.00	$0.00	$26.00	$15.67	$15.00
Gas/Heating Oil	$35.00	$31.00	$38.00	$34.67	$35.00
Insurance	$94.00	$94.00	$94.00	$94.00	$94.00
Groceries	$428.00	$465.00	$453.00	$448.67	$450.00
Miscellaneous	$23.00	$45.00	$36.00	$34.67	$35.00
Daycare	$125.00	$125.00	$125.00	$125.00	$125.00
Health Club	$52.00	$52.00	$52.00	$52.00	$52.00
Entertainment	$86.00	$48.00	$65.00	$66.33	$65.00
Other				$0.00	$0.00
Other				$0.00	$0.00
TOTAL BUDGET DOLLARS	$2,026.00	$2,014.00	$2,048.00	$2,029.33	$2,028.00
DEFICIT DOLLARS					
Credit Card #1	$135.00	$138.00	$120.00	$131.00	$125.00
Credit Card #2	$0.00	$0.00	$0.00	$0.00	$0.00
Auto Loan #1	$360.00	$360.00	$360.00	$360.00	$360.00
Auto Loan #2	$308.00	$308.00	$308.00	$308.00	$308.00
Other				$0.00	$0.00
Other				$0.00	$0.00
Other				$0.00	$0.00
TOTAL DEFICIT DOLLARS	$803.00	$806.00	$788.00	$799.00	$793.00
TOTAL DOLLARS SPENT	$3,079.00	$3,070.00	$3,086.00	$3,078.33	$3,600.00

YOUR MONTHLY BUDGET FOR YEAR BEGINNING				January 1995			
ITEM	BUDGET	MONTH 1	MONTH 2	MONTH 3	MONTH 4	MONTH 5	MONTH 6
PROSPERITY DOLLARS							
Reserve Account	$250.00	$250.00	$250.00	$250.00	$250.00	$250.00	$250.00
Retirement Account	$400.00	$400.00	$400.00	$400.00	$400.00	$400.00	$400.00
College Fund	$129.00	$129.00	$129.00	$129.00	$129.00	$129.00	$129.00
TOTAL PROSPERITY DOLLARS	$779.00	$779.00	$779.00	$779.00	$779.00	$779.00	$779.00
BUDGET DOLLARS							
Mortgage/Rent	$1,047.00	$1,047.00	$1,047.00	$1,047.00	$1,047.00	$1,047.00	$1,047.00
Telephone	$45.00	$42.00	$55.00	$38.00	$44.00	$46.00	$35.00
Electricity	$65.00	$63.00	$66.00	$65.00	$68.00	$61.00	$65.00
Water/Sewer	$15.00	$13.00	$16.00	$15.00	$18.00	$13.00	$15.00
Gas/Heating Oil	$35.00	$35.00	$38.00	$38.00	$32.00	$30.00	$35.00
Insurance	$94.00	$94.00	$94.00	$94.00	$94.00	$94.00	$94.00
Groceries	$450.00	$438.00	$461.00	$447.00	$450.00	$425.00	$488.00
Miscellaneous	$35.00	$23.00	$25.00	$40.00	$38.00	$60.00	$35.00
Daycare	$125.00	$125.00	$125.00	$125.00	$125.00	$125.00	$125.00
Health Club	$52.00	$52.00	$52.00	$52.00	$52.00	$52.00	$52.00
Entertainment	$65.00	$57.00	$48.00	$73.00	$65.00	$68.00	$65.00
Other	$0.00						
Other	$0.00						
TOTAL BUDGET DOLLARS	$2,028.00	$1,989.00	$2,027.00	$2,034.00	$2,033.00	$2,021.00	$2,056.00
DEFICIT DOLLARS							
Credit Card #1	$125.00	$133.00	$125.00	$125.00	$120.00	$125.00	$135.00
Credit Card #2	$0.00						
Auto Loan #1	$360.00	$360.00	$360.00	$360.00	$360.00	$360.00	$360.00
Auto Loan #2	$308.00	$308.00	$308.00	$308.00	$308.00	$308.00	$308.00
Other	$0.00						
Other	$0.00						
Other	$0.00						
TOTAL DEFICIT DOLLARS	$793.00	$801.00	$793.00	$793.00	$788.00	$793.00	$803.00
TOTAL DOLLARS SPENT	$3,600.00	$3,569.00	$3,599.00	$3,606.00	$3,600.00	$3,593.00	$3,638.00
BUDGET SURPLUS/(DEFICIT)	$0.00	$31.00	$1.00	($6.00)	$0.00	$7.00	($38.00)

YOUR MONTHLY BUDGET FOR YEAR BEGINNING			January 1995				Page 2	
ITEM	BUDGET	MONTH 7	MONTH 8	MONTH 9	MONTH 10	MONTH 11	MONTH 12	
PROSPERITY DOLLARS								
Reserve Account	$250.00							
Retirement Account	$400.00							
College Fund	$129.00							
TOTAL PROSPERITY DOLLARS	$779.00	$0.00	$0.00	$0.00	$0.00	$0.00	$0.00	
BUDGET DOLLARS								
Mortgage/Rent	$1,047.00							
Telephone	$45.00							
Electricity	$65.00							
Water/Sewer	$15.00							
Gas/Heating Oil	$35.00							
Insurance	$94.00							
Groceries	$450.00							
Miscellaneous	$35.00							
Daycare	$125.00							
Health Club	$52.00							
Entertainment	$65.00							
Other	$0.00							
Other	$0.00							
TOTAL BUDGET DOLLARS	$2,028.00	$0.00	$0.00	$0.00	$0.00	$0.00	$0.00	
DEFICIT DOLLARS								
Credit Card #1	$125.00							
Credit Card #2	$0.00							
Auto Loan #1	$360.00							
Auto Loan #2	$308.00							
Other	$0.00							
Other	$0.00							
Other	$0.00							
TOTAL DEFICIT DOLLARS	$793.00	$0.00	$0.00	$0.00	$0.00	$0.00	$0.00	
TOTAL DOLLARS SPENT	$3,600.00	$0.00	$0.00	$0.00	$0.00	$0.00	$0.00	
BUDGET SURPLUS/(DEFICIT)	$0.00	$0.00	$0.00	$0.00	$0.00	$0.00	$0.00	

YOUR RETIREMENT NEST EGG

Number of Years Remaining Before Retirement	29
Amount of Money Currently Saved for Retirement	$3,500
Annual Investment Earnings Rate	7%
Monthly Savings for Retirement Account	$250

Monthly Contribution	Retirement Nest Egg
$250	$308,000
$300	$364,300
$350	$420,700
$400	$477,000
$450	$533,300
$500	$589,600
$550	$645,900
$600	$702,200
$650	$758,500
$700	$814,800
$750	$871,100
$800	$927,400
$850	$983,700
$900	$1,040,000
$950	$1,096,400
$1,000	$1,152,700
$1,050	$1,209,000
$1,100	$1,265,300
$1,150	$1,321,600

YOUR CHILD'S COLLEGE FUND

Number of Years Until Child Enters College	16
Amount of Money Currently Saved for College	$0
Annual Investment Earnings Rate	7%
Monthly Savings for College Fund	$129

Monthly Contribution	Child's College Fund
$129	$45,400
$179	$63,100
$229	$80,700
$279	$98,300
$329	$115,900
$379	$133,500
$429	$151,100
$479	$168,700
$529	$186,300
$579	$204,000
$629	$221,600
$679	$239,200
$729	$256,800
$779	$274,400
$829	$292,000
$879	$309,600
$929	$327,300
$979	$344,900
$1,029	$362,500

APPENDIX B

Will Module

Your Will

Objective: To provide you with a simple-to-use word processing template of a legal will. You only need to fill-in the blanks and print out the completed will.

Instructions: The files provided on your diskette are directly compatible with Word Perfect or Word, or can be imported into other popular word processing programs by using the ASCII file and following your own user's manual instructions for loading an ASCII text file into your word processing software.

Software Requirements	File Name
Word Perfect 5.1 or higher	WILL 1.WP
Word 2.0 or higher	WILL 2.DOC
ASCII File	WILL3.TXT

Once you have the file up and running, simply follow the specific functions of your own software to enter data, change the format, save or print the *Your Will* template.

Your Will is a template of a legal will. All you have to do is fill-in the blanks, print it out, and sign it with three witnesses present. The witnesses (who should *not* also be beneficiaries of the will) must also sign the will in your presence.

If a portion of the template does not apply to your particular circumstances, here is what you do: If, for example, you do not have any children, then in each of the blanks where it asks for each child's name, you simply type DOES NOT APPLY.

The template is also designed so that you can eliminate whole pages that do not pertain to your particular circumstance. For example, if you do not have any children, you simply eliminate the page headed LEGAL GUARDIAN from the final copy of your will.

The template has room for you to name seven bene-ficiaries. If you have more than that, simply re-enter the program and fill in the information for additional beneficiaries. Be sure to adjust the corresponding beneficiary number.

Be sure to fill-in page numbers at the bottom of each page, and be sure to mark your initials at the bottom of each page.

Finally, as a rule, it is a good idea to create only one signed copy of your will. If you plan to give copies of your will to your executor/executrix and to each of your beneficiaries, it is best to give them *unsigned* copies to eliminate any potential confusion during probate.

If you decide to keep the signed copy of your will in a safety deposit box at a bank, be sure the bank has instructions on file that will allow your spouse and/or your executor/executrix to have immediate access to your will in the event of your death. Without explicit instructions, the safety deposit box could conceivably be sealed until the probate process begins.

Instructions for the Codicil Template: If you need to change something in your will, you must create a codicil to your will. The CODICIL template works the same way as the template for *Your Will*: simply fill-in the blanks, print it out, and sign it in front of three witnesses. Note that these three witnesses do not have to be the same three who witnessed the signing of your will.

You must state which codicil this is (first, second, or whichever). A blank space is provided.

In the space where you revoke a portion of your will, you *must* quote exactly the portion you are revoking.

LAST WILL AND TESTAMENT

My full legal name is:_____
       (first)   (middle)   (last)

I have also been known by the following name(s):

   1._____
           (first)   (middle)   (last)

   2._____
           (first)   (middle)   (last)

My date of birth is:_____
           (month)   (day)   (year)

My Social Security number is:_____-____-_____

I am married to:_____ __
           (first)   (middle)   (last)

His/Her Social Security number is:_____-____-_____

We were married:_____
           (month)   (day)   (year)

I used to be married to:_____
           (first)   (middle)   (last)

We were married from _____ to _____
                       (wedding date)   (final divorce date)

His/Her Social Security number is:_____-____-_____

I am the parent of the following children:

1._____   _____
 (first)   (middle)   (last)   (date of birth)
2._____   _____
 (first)   (middle)   (last)   (date of birth)
3._____   _____
 (first)   (middle)   (last)   (date of birth)
4._____   _____
 (first)   (middle)   (last)   (date of birth)
5._____   _____
 (first)   (middle)   (last)   (date of birth)

Page _____ of _____   (initial here): _____

PROPERTY AND POLICIES

I own the following life insurance policy (or policies):

1._____
   (insurance company)   (policy number)   (amount of policy)

_____
(beneficiary/beneficiaries listed on policy)

2._____
   (insurance company)   (policy number)   (amount of policy)

_____
(beneficiary/beneficiaries listed on policy)

I own/control the following property/accounts in joint tenancy:

1._____
   (description of property/account)

_____   _____-____-_____
(name of joint tenant)   (S.S.#)

2._____
   (description of property/account)

_____   _____-____-_____
(name of joint tenant)   (S.S.#)

3._____
   (description of property/account)

_____   _____-____-_____
(name of joint tenant)   (S.S.#)

4._____
   (description of property/account)

_____   _____-____-_____
(name of joint tenant)   (S.S.#)

5._____
   (description of property/account)

_____   _____-____-_____
(name of joint tenant)   (S.S.#)

Page _____ of _____   (initial here): _____

BENEFICIARIES

Here is a list of my beneficiaries and what each is to receive:

1._____   _____-____-_____
   (first)   (middle)   (last)   (S.S.#)

Description of gift(s):_____

_____

2._____   _____-____-_____
   (first)   (middle)   (last)   (S.S.#)

Description of gift(s):_____

_____

3._____   _____-____-_____
   (first)   (middle)   (last)   (S.S.#)

Description of gift(s):_____

_____

4._____   _____-____-_____
   (first)   (middle)   (last)   (S.S.#)

Description of gift(s):_____

_____

5._____   _____-____-_____
   (first)   (middle)   (last)   (S.S.#)

Description of gift(s):_____

_____

6._____   _____-____-_____
   (first)   (middle)   (last)   (S.S.#)

Description of gift(s):_____

_____

7._____   _____-____-_____
   (first)   (middle)   (last)   (S.S.#)

Description of gift(s):_____

_____

Page _____ of _____   (initial here): _____

If any of the above beneficiaries do not survive me by 30 days, then these are my instructions:

1. For beneficiary #1:_____

_____

_____

2. For beneficiary #2:_____

_____

_____

3. For beneficiary #3:_____

_____

_____

4. For beneficiary #4:_____

_____

_____

5. For beneficiary #5:_____

_____

_____

6. For beneficiary #6:_____

_____

_____

7. For beneficiary #7:_____

_____

_____

If any of the above beneficiaries do not survive me by 30 days, and any of the above alternate instructions cannot be carried out, I leave it to my executor/executrix to dispense with the property in question.

Page _____ of _____   (initial here): _____

EXECUTOR/EXECUTRIX

I hereby name as the executor/executrix of my estate:

_____
(first)   (middle)   (last)

_____-_____-_____
(Social Security #)

If for any reason, he/she cannot fulfill the responsibilities of executor/executrix, I hereby name as alternate executor/executrix:

_____
(first)   (middle)   (last)

_____-_____-_____
(Social Security #)

I expect my executor/executrix to carry out my wishes stated in this will. If, for whatever reason, that is not possible, I leave it to my executor's/executrix's judgment to oversee the administration of my estate. My executor/executrix enjoys any and all legal powers vested in him/her by state and federal law.

For acting as executor/executrix of my estate, I hereby leave him/her the following:

Description:_____

_____

_____

_____

Page _____ of _____   (initial here): _____

LEGAL GUARDIAN

If my spouse and I should die simultaneously, and any of our children are legal minors and/or disabled at the time of our death, I hereby name as legal guardian(s) of those children:

1._____ _____ _____-____-_____
  (first)   (middle)   (last)   (S.S.#)

2._____ _____-____-_____
  (first)   (middle)   (last)   (S.S.#)

If, for any reason, he/she/they are unable to perform the duties of legal guardianship, I hereby name as alternate guardian(s):

1._____ _____-____-_____
  (first)   (middle)   (last)   (S.S.#)

2._____ _____-____-_____
  (first)   (middle)   (last)   (S.S.#)

These are my special instructions regarding procedures and/or accounts to be used for the rearing and/or care of the children:

_____

_____

_____

_____

_____

For acting as legal guardian(s), I hereby leave him/her/them the following:

Description:_____

_____

NOTE: If my spouse and I do die simultaneously, it shall be conclusively presumed for the purposes of this will that I survived my spouse.

Page _____ of _____   (initial here): _____

SUBSCRIPTION

My legal residence is:_____
　　　　　　　　　　(number)　　　(street)　　　(apt. #)

_____
(city)　　　　　　　(county)　　　　　(state)　　　　(zip)

I hereby declare that I am of sound mind and body, and that I am signing this document without any undo influence.

_____
(signature)　　　　　　　　　　　　　(date)

WITNESSES

We, the undersigned, do declare that this is the last will and testament of

_____ and that we were present when he/she signed this
(first)　　　(middle)　　　(last)
　　　　　　　　　　　　　　　　　　　document.

1._____　　_____
　(witness #1 signature)　　　　　　　　　(date)

_____　　_____-____-_____
(legal residence of witness #1)　　　　　　(S.S.#)

2._____　　_____
　(witness #2 signature)　　　　　　　　　(date)

_____　　_____-____-_____
(legal residence of witness #2)　　　　　　(S.S.#)

3._____　　_____
　(witness #3 signature)　　　　　　　　　(date)

_____　　_____-____-_____
(legal residence of witness #3)　　　　　　(S.S.#)

Page _____ of _____　　　　　　　　　　　　(initial here): _____

CODICIL

My full legal name is:_____
            (first)   (middle)   (last)

My Social Security number is:_____-_____-_____

I declare this to be the _____ codicil to my will dated:_____

I revoke the portion of my will that provided:
_____
_____
_____

I add the following provision:
_____
_____
_____

I hereby declare that I am of sound mind and body, and that I am signing this codicil without any undue influence.

Signature:_____
                                    (date)

My legal residence is:_____
                (number)   (street)   (apt. #)

_____
(city)   (county)   (state)   (zip)

We, the undersigned, hereby declare this to be the _____ codicil to the will of

_____, and that he/she signed it in our presence.
        (first)   (middle)   (last)

Witness #1:_____ _____
                (signature)   (date)

_____ _____-____-_____
(legal residence)   (S.S.#)

Witness #2:_____ _____
                (signature)   (date)

_____ _____-____-_____
(legal residence)   (S.S.#)

Witness #3:_____ _____
                (signature)   (date)

_____ _____-____-_____
(legal residence)   (S.S.#)

APPENDIX C

Consumer Expenditure Survey

CONSUMER EXPENDITURE SURVEY, 1992

Age of reference person: Average annual expenditures and characteristics.

Item	Under 25	25–34
Number of consumer units (in thousands)....................	7,676	20,763
Consumer unit characteristics:		
Income before taxes[1]...	$15,197	$33,124
Averages:		
Age of reference person......................................	21.6	29.8
Number of persons in consumer unit...............	1.9	2.8
Number of earners..	1.2	1.5
Number of vehicles	1.2	1.8
Percent homeowner...	11	42
Average annual expenditures	$17,258	$29,554
Food	2,621	4,218
Food at home...	1,440	2,486
Cereals and bakery products	211	388
Meats, poultry, fish, and eggs.....................	350	631
Dairy products	167	287
Fruits and vegetables....................................	226	370
Other food at home......................................	486	810
Food away from home......................................	1,181	1,732
Alcoholic beverages	356	365
Housing..	5,135	10,018
Shelter...	3,148	6,132
Owned dwellings...	363	3,146
Rented dwellings...	2,656	2,817
Other lodging...	129	169
Utilities, fuels, and public services....................	1,024	1,797
Household operations......................................	141	579
Housekeeping supplies	170	365
Household furnishing and equipment	652	1,145
Apparel and services...	1,267	1,842
Transportation...	3,622	5,376
Vehicle purchases (net outlay)	1,743	2,355
Gasoline and motor oil	649	994
Other vehicle expenses....................................	1,086	1,772
Public transportation.......................................	144	255
Health care..	416	1,053
Entertainment..	928	1,569
Personal care products and services.......................	253	361
Reading	73	142
Education	833	305
Tobacco products and smoking supplies...............	220	278
Miscellaneous..	408	780
Cash contributions...	124	428
Personal insurance and pensions............................	1,003	2,821
Life and other personal insurance....................	50	238
Pensions and Social Security............................	953	2,583

[1]Components of income and taxes are derived from "complete income reporters" only.
source: Bureau of Labor Statistics

35–44	45–54	55–64	65 and Over
21,837	15,754	12,225	21,763
$43,923	$46,186	$37,610	$20,890
39.4	49.0	59.4	74.4
3.2	2.8	2.4	1.7
1.7	1.8	1.4	.4
2.2	2.5	2.2	1.5
63	74	79	77
$37,196	$37,427	$31,704	$20,616
5,218	5,233	4,354	3,198
3,201	3,102	2,833	2,211
490	483	440	354
832	822	753	579
380	350	303	247
494	485	490	416
1,005	961	847	615
2,017	2,131	1,521	987
352	299	321	159
12,120	11,036	9,436	6,733
7,215	6,299	5,105	3,241
4,926	4,406	3,514	1,978
1,901	1,313	1,016	1,039
387	580	575	223
2,232	2,375	2,255	1,816
664	393	374	474
507	560	450	413
1,502	1,409	1,252	789
2,210	2,245	1,631	882
6,228	6,755	5,684	3,290
2,584	2,772	2,329	1,289
1,165	1,269	1,046	621
2,155	2,364	1,945	1,122
324	350	364	257
1,570	1,646	1,993	2,474
2,041	1,896	1,587	754
461	481	408	306
183	204	188	144
533	809	282	93
326	376	310	147
985	982	788	484
938	1,208	1,620	1,227
4,030	4,256	3,103	724
456	531	491	259
3,574	3,725	2,612	465

INDEX